Pathways to College Success

Katherine Costa
Jason Bradley Pennington

Nashua Community College

www.kendallhunt.com
Send all inquiries to:
4050 Westmark Drive
Dubuque, IA 52004-1840

ISBN 978-1-4652-0850-7

Printed in the United States of America
10 9 8 7 6 5 4 3

Contents

Chapter 1

Week-One Field Survival Guide

INTRODUCTION

Welcome to college.

Making this decision represents a major life choice. For some, this is perhaps the first life choice you've ever made. However one views the decision to go to college, it is a big deal. Your life in many ways will be shaped by what happens to you here—how you perform, how you view yourself, and what you will be doing in the future. Since you have chosen to be here, this book will assume that you are here because you want to be here.

Period.

With consideration of those students feeling like attending college was not their choice (we know you're out there), all students who pay for the privilege of attending class need to be prepared to have their ideas of what it means to be a student challenged. Your world is now automatically different than before, and it is important to recognize that you will need to adapt to this very new environment. For some this takes a semester. For some it may take several years. Everybody experiences college differently, and being an effective college student means that you must to learn to become an effective college student. This book addresses this seismic shift in your life.

If you feel you are in college against your will, you may want to consider other plans, routes, options, etc. For those of you with parents who think college is the only path for you at this point in your lives, but you do not share your thoughts, show them the following sentence.

> *This experience needs to be yours, and yours only.*

In other words, you are doing this for yourself, or there's a really good chance that you will not do it at all. College is too expensive, not just from a dollars sense, to not be doing it for yourself.

Now that we have that out of the way, there are many questions to ponder about the value of higher education and what meaning the experience will have for you before taking the journey down this particular pathway. Yet, there is one standout question, and only you can answer it.

> *Why are you here?*

Dig deep in considering this question. Many students would automatically say, "to get an education." Well, duh. Such a statement is broad and does not give an idea as to what specifically you want out of this experience. Besides, the whole idea of education could mean various things. If this is your answer, think of how you would define what education means. Other students might say, "money, money, money, show me the money." Yes. It is true that college graduates earn on average more than $900,000 (CITE) more in their lifetimes than those with just a high school credential or equivalency. Most higher paying jobs come with the requirement of earned college degree. However, a college credential is not a guaranteed path to your choice career. Think of something else. Think of something unique, or something other students may not have thought about. Think about your own definition of the word education. Think about what you have to offer this experience, not what this experience has to offer you.

This question will be explored at various times during this course. It is something that may evolve day-to-day, week-to-week, semester-to-semester, year-to-year. As you change and experience more, this too will most likely change.

Apart from exploring why you are here and what you want out of this experience, Chapter 1 starts the discussion that will be carried throughout the book on what it takes to be successful in college. To be successful, you need to recognize six not-so-secret secrets to college success right from the get go. That is why we call this chapter "The Week One Survival Guide." We do understand that this experience is new, and when an experience is new it may be difficult to think about what the best course of action is when you are being exposed to so many different ideas and concepts. By no means are these six not-so-secret secrets all there is to college, but they can be helpful in getting you started on the right track.

The six not-so-secret secrets (more on these later)

1. Show up
2. Challenge your notion of hard and intensive study
3. Commit to putting this notion into practice and maintain it
4. Be motivated and proactive
5. Get to know folks
6. Embrace change, as college will be nothing like your previous educational experience

Oh, we forgot one: have fun. This is not just from the personal/social sense. Learn to have fun with learning. We're not suggesting that you learn to enjoy long lectures, per se, but we are suggesting that you at least embrace the idea of learning about things you do not necessarily see as being helpful to your long-term plans. It's imperative that you attempt to get something out of each class and enter the classroom thinking that you will.

> *College, more often than not, is not about what you are learning about a subject, but what you are learning about yourself through the experience.*

You will be seeing a lot of material throughout college, at all levels, that does not seem to be particularly applicable to your degree. That does not assume that it's meaningless to you. Chapter 1 and the subsequent chapters delve into this more specifically, and in greater detail.

For now, welcome. Enjoy. And, if you have a question, PLEASE ASK SOMEBODY.

THE BEGINNING

Getting to Class

Finding the classroom tends to be the most stressful thing about week one for more students, and if you have felt this stress already, great! You're a normal college student. If you haven't, then you too are probably a normal college student.

Getting to class on time is certainly important, so many students arrive for the first class 45 minutes early because they don't want to be "that person," AKA the person who walks in late on day one. But, if you're late on the first day, big deal. Nobody is going to point out your incompetence as a student. That includes the professor.

If you are lost, and it is very easy to get lost on college campuses big and small, it is okay to duck into an office on campus to ask for assistance. This is a level of interdependence that you may have never had to employ or thought to employ, but campus staff and faculty are there to help. Taking the initiative to ask (even if it's for directions) is really important in college, as asking for help is something college students should expect to do often during their academic career.

Textbooks

No Hard or Fast Rules to Using Textbooks

Much is made about the cost and roles of textbooks in college.

Why are they so expensive?
Is it important to have the book?
Is it true that reading is necessary to be successful in the classroom?

Considering these questions, be prepared for the following earth shattering revelation:

College is a lot less structured than high school.

That's not to suggest that courses are not well structured, or organized. They typically are. What it does mean, however, is that your professors will have different teaching styles and methods. There is no certification process for teaching college, and because of this lack of a factory approach to crafting teachers in college, there is no easy answer to the questions listed above.

Although there are no hard or fast rules to college and textbook use, there are some essential rules regarding textbooks that are worth considering when taking college classes.

RULE #1: Have all of your books purchased prior to walking into class on day 1

Let's start with the cost of textbooks. Yes. They are expensive. Nobody will dispute this. When you get to college and you think the tuition bill is high, spending another $450 on textbooks can be, gulp . . . difficult to stomach. But this is the going rate for being in college in 2012. Some fields will require textbooks that are more expensive than other fields. In general, textbooks in Mathematics, Science, Law, Business, World Language, and technical fields like Engineering, Architecture, and Medicine will be considerably more expensive than say in Humanities-based fields. This isn't always the case, of course, but this is a general truth.

Despite the expense of textbooks, having them is part of being a college student. Since college is not a requirement (e.g., your parents will not face criminal charges if you do not attend college), students are responsible for having access to all textbooks and course materials for all classes taken. As a best practice, you should have access to all of your books prior to the first day of class, as students who have obtained copies of their textbooks by day one are much more likely to successfully complete the class than those who have not.

RULE #2: Be prepared to read from day 1 onward

Although there is no rule to how college courses are taught and how instructors manage in-class and outside of class work, one thing is true: They will want to hit the ground running.

You should be prepared to have assigned work from the first day of class, and it is usually in the form of assigned readings. In all likelihood, you will be required to have all textbook readings done ahead of the next class meeting, as your instructors may look to discuss the readings in lecture. They may look for you to participate in a classwide discussion on the readings, or they may opt to assign homework directly from the text.

Reading assignments can vary, but most reading assignments involve covering 60+ pages every week during a standard 16-week semester. Many instructors will look to cover an entire textbook. Not having your textbooks going into the first day of class may undermine your ability to succeed over the course of the semester, as it is very difficult to make up for lost readings. Just like missing class, being off track with the readings can be very hard to overcome—think that instead of reading 60 pages per week, you are required to read 120 because you were unable to complete the first week of reading assignments. Also consider that some instructors do like to give unannounced quizzes on the reading after the first week of classes to gauge who is doing the readings and to what level of attention they are giving them.

RULE #3: Complete the readings even if they do not seem relevant to what is being covered in class

As a warning, assigned textbooks may not serve as the centerpieces to the courses you take. In some classes, you will not discuss what is covered in the textbook, or what is covered early in the semester may come out in bits and pieces as the semester progresses. On the other hand, some instructors will base their lessons directly on the textbook readings. The main purpose of textbooks is to supplement what your instructor is teaching in the classroom, or to give further clarity to concepts covered in class. Do not, however, have the expectation that what you are reading in the book will overlap with what's being covered in the classroom.

The readings in your textbooks may be long. They may or may not pique your interest. They certainly may not seem relevant to what's being covered in class, but this illustrates a major difference between high school and college. In college, textbooks are not seen as providing a complete learning experience. Students learn from faculty interaction. They also learn from what they read in their textbooks. In high school, class material was likely driven by the textbooks issued to students on day one.

THE ADVISER SAYS: It is your responsibility to purchase books prior to the start of the class. If you are a recipient of federal financial aid, ask your financial aid counselor about the possibility of receiving book vouchers. If you have enough money available beyond the cost of tuition, they will allow you to purchase books with a voucher before they cut the check for money additional to tuition.

What if I cannot afford to purchase the book?

In some circumstances, your instructor may put a textbook on reserve in the library. This is a way to manage not being able to afford the book during the first month of class, but it can become cumbersome as the semester progresses to continually access the book in the library. Books on reserve are available to students to look at in the library, but they cannot be checked out. This means that these books are not accessible at all times, like owning your textbooks would be, and because all students could access these books in the library, a student is not guaranteed to access the book at all.

Making copies of pages out of books is not an option, as federal copyright laws prohibit such action, unless the book is in the public domain. Chances are your textbooks are not in the public domain. You will want to avoid asking your instructors for copies out of the textbooks. Many will see this as a breach of ethics.

Where can I purchase my books?

Books are available for purchase in the school bookstore. Students should be able to access a book list from their school bookstores. In addition to this, federal law dictates that all schools are required to provide students title information, author information, edition information, and ISBN for all textbooks required for all classes. Access to this information would allow students to make textbook purchases online.

THE ADVISER SAYS: At Nashua Community College students can find relevant textbook information on Student Information Systems, under "View Detailed Course Schedule."

It is important to note that although purchasing textbooks online may lower the cost, you must be an informed consumer. By purchasing textbooks at your bookstore, you remove any of the variables that can cause trouble when ordering books online. The books are in house, they are delivered directly to you, and you know that your money is going to the company that runs your campus bookstore. There is credibility in that.

When you order online, you must, MUST ensure that the vendor from which you are purchasing your books is a reputable e-business. If a price seems too good to be true, it probably is. When you order online, you run the risk of delayed delivery, or delivery that never happens at all. Some places will advertise that they have a book in stock, and three weeks later, you may get notification that the book was backordered or out of stock to begin with.

The Course Catalog

Course catalogs are published every year and, like the syllabus, represent a contract of sorts between the student and the school. When a student enters a college or university and declares a major, she will follow the major's program requirements as outlined in the course catalog that was published during the academic year the major was declared. For example, if a new student is looking to take on a psychology degree and enters school in the Fall 2012, she will be following the requirements of the program as published in the course catalog for the semester she entered. Those are the requirements she will have to complete to graduate. Even if her program goes through curriculum changes, she will be pursing degree requirements for Fall 2012 because it follows the catalog published the semester she entered. If a student changes majors at any point during her time in college, she would then follow the program requirements of the catalog published for the academic year the major change occurred.

THE ADVISER SAYS: It is essential that you keep a copy of the course catalog published when you enter your degree program and to use it to keep track of the courses you have taken toward degree completion. You must take the primary role in your track toward degree completion. This will eliminate complications when you are ready to graduate if you are working with an academic or faculty adviser, as you will have two sets of eyes on what you have done and what you have left.

In addition to program requirements, the course catalog will include course descriptions for all courses offered by the school. Course descriptions are typically a brief summary of what a course entails. The catalog will also include policy information on grade point average, graduation, and academic standing, among other things.

The Student Handbook/Planner

Many schools supply student handbooks during orientation or first-year experience classes, and this book is essential. It is issued every year by the school, and you should not just put it to the side, burn it, throw it in the trash, or file it under your bed. Place it somewhere you can access it on a whim. Yes. It's a pretty dull, boring book, but it does detail the policies of the school, and you should gain a basic knowledge of these or, at least, have easy access to it so you can look up the policies. In addition to the policies, it will outline the Add/Drop policy for classes (which may be applicable to you this week, as students change classes all of the time) and will give the important dates in the academic calendar. These dates may include when midterms and finals are, when the last day to drop classes without academic penalty is, and when course registration for the next semester opens. Again, you should have a basic knowledge of these, as it is your responsibility to know when things happen during the semester.

Many colleges, including NCC, have incorporated a planner into the handbook. This planner, like any planner you would pick up at the store, has a calendar for jotting in appointments and upcoming tasks. This calendar may include all important academic dates (or at least you could write them in), and it allows you to plan out test dates and when major assignments are due. If your student handbook does not have a planner, consider buying one, if you know you would use it. Planners can be really helpful at giving you a visual aid on a week-to-week basis, so you will know what weeks are heavier work-wise than others. You can plug those dates in when you receive course syllabi and course calendars for all of your classes.

Syllabus and Course Calendar

There are many important documents you will receive in your college courses, like reading questions, assignments, testing parameters, etc. None of them, however, are as essential as the document you receive on day one of class: the course syllabus and calendar.

View the course syllabus as your contract with the instructor for the semester. In general, the syllabus and course calendar are the management tools for the class and together they:

- Provide a course description, which is a general summary of the course you are taking (note: everything in the course description must be covered in a course)
- Outline the course outcomes or what you will be expected to learn during the semester
- Define the course objectives of what the course aims to cover
- Specifically define what assignments are covered in class
- Give the grading scale or weights for assignments, tests, papers, journals, practicals, participation, etc.
- Generally explain what major assignments will entail
- Lay out the instructor's and the school's expectations/policies on attendance, tardiness, behavior, work submission, grades, late work, testing, grade appeals, and quality of work, among many other things
- Provide dates for all readings, assignments, journals, tests, paper submissions, practicals, and what will generally be covered in class on a week-by-week basis

It is the student's responsibility solely to ensure that he/she has access to the syllabus. It is distributed to students on the first day of a class, and if a student does not make it to the first class, for whatever reason (tuition issues, late registration, work, other commitments, etc.), it is the student's responsibility to obtain the syllabus as soon as possible. Remember, as soon as this document is passed out to students, the clock is ticking on the semester. Your first assignments will be outlined in the course calendar and they need to be done ahead of the second class, whether you have the syllabus or not.

Once you receive the syllabus, your instructor may go over it with the class, or they may point out a couple points of importance and have you read the rest. Read this document thoroughly, and keep a copy that can be accessed in the classroom or during study time. This syllabus should not be too far away from you at all times during a semester. Good personal organization helps out tremendously. Go purchase a 24-cent folder from your local stationary or multipurpose store and keep the course syllabus and all assignments in it for the duration of the semester.

Easy access is a must, and if all your instructor relies on is a hard copy (i.e., she is not posting one electronically in Blackboard or will not email it to you if you ask), losing a course syllabus is not an option. You will want to look at the course calendar for each course at least once per week, preferably at the beginning of each week. This will give you perspective on what is due and when it is due, as instructors rarely issue reminders of due dates during class. She may just expect you to submit your work when the syllabus says. Knowing due dates will also shape your study and time management strategies during a semester.

THE ADVISER SAYS: In college, it feels like due dates for major assignments and tests fall around the same time for multiple classes. I assure you that instructors do not get together and schedule tests and major assignments for the same times during the semester, but because of the structure of a semester, with a midterm and final, it just seems like they do.

You should consider looking at the course calendars for all of your courses, side-by-side, during the first week of the semester to determine what weeks major assignments are due. You will have clarity on when your extremely heavy weeks are going to be. Not only does this help with time management, but it helps with stress management as well. Knowing early on what to expect week in and week out gives you the advantage of mentally preparing for when you will have to ramp up your time commitment for each class.

UNDERSTANDING E-RESOURCES

Colleges and universities are continually increasing the number of electronic resources used as learning tools. Student email has become the primary tool for communication between faculty and students, tools like Student Information Systems (SIS) or Pipeline are being used for everything from giving final grades to students to being the primary billing method for all school-related expenses, and online tools like Blackboard or Moodle are being incorporated more and more at schools as online classrooms and course management tools. In addition to this, social media is rapidly emerging into the classroom. For example, Twitter has emerged in the classroom as a real-time event documentation tool.

Many of you are beyond familiar with the cyberspace and social media, and you may have been using computers since you were Kindergarteners, or sooner! Those of you who are not as familiar with computers, the expectation is that you will be functional relatively soon, as you will be expected to access these types of resources at any time. If a professor sends an entire class an email about a change in test time or posted an announcement about a class cancellation on Blackboard, it is your responsibility to get the information. It is a good practice to check your student email accounts as much as you would your personal email. If that's not possible, you should be accessing it once per day, at the very least.

THE SCHOOL'S IT GURU SAYS: Your student email account is most likely tied to the online classroom application used by your school, so if your instructor posts an announcement or sends an email to your entire class, you will receive the message in your student email.

THE ADVISER SAYS: You may have to keep different usernames and passwords for each application your school offers. Keeping these names and passwords in one safe place is essential.

Student Information Systems (SIS)

The Community College System of New Hampshire uses SIS as the house for the personal and student information (i.e., grades, schedules, bills, financial aid information, etc.) the school has on file for you.

By this point of class, you should have already accessed your course schedule on SIS. You may have even accessed textbook information on SIS. You will be using SIS rather extensively through the semester.

Under student information is registration, billing, financial aid information, and academic performance information.

Registration

You accessed your schedule by clicking into the registration screen. You can find textbook information here and, by your third semester, you would be able to register for classes online.

Billing

All tuition expenses including credit hour charges, lab fees, fines, fees, and financial hold information can be found under the billing link.

Financial Aid Information

This section outlines exactly what you are eligible for, what types of aid you receive (i.e., Pell grants, unsubsidized and subsidized Stafford loans, scholarships, etc.), and how it applies to your tuition. Accessing your financial aid information here is quick and it provides a bird's eye view of how your aid applies to your education.

Academic Performance Information

There are three areas that are important to note when discussing academic performance.

1. Your midterm grades are posted to this section of SIS usually around week eight of the semester. The grades will only appear if you are receiving a C– or lower in a class at the time of the midterm. This is designed to give you a definitive idea of how you're doing in your classes, and it gives you time to make decisions about your academic direction if you are struggling in a class prior to the midterm.
2. Your final grades are posted to this section. This is important to note, as you will not receive your grades in the mail, as you may have in high school or your previous educational experience. Typically, your grades will be available about one week after the last day of final exams.
3. The third thing you can access in this section is your unofficial transcript. This will detail your education in its entirety, including the courses you've taken, courses you are registered for, the number of credits successfully completed, grade point averages for each semester taken, and your cumulative grade point average (CGPA), which is the average GPA for all semesters completed at NCC. You may not submit this to other schools as an official record of your academics upon transferring, but it is a way for you to track your progress through your degree program.

THE ADVISER SAYS: You should print out a copy of your unofficial transcript before meeting with your adviser to select your next classes. You should also use it to track the courses you've taken in your degree program. Showing your adviser that you have a command of your academic direction is (a) impressive and (b) indicative of where the responsibility for school management resides—with you, not your adviser.

Student Email

As mentioned, this will be the primary way the school and your professors can communicate with you, and it is essential that you not only log in to access your email, but also send email from this account to others on campus when necessary. There are so many filters on the official email accounts of faculty and staff that it is possible that email sent from personal accounts goes directly to SPAM folders. Therefore, if you need to email your instructor to let her know that you will not be in class due to a family emergency, you will want to do that through your student email to ensure timely delivery.

At NCC, your student email address is a little more complex than something you might set up at gmail or yahoo. Your email prefix will be your first initial and full last name with three randomly selected numbers. The suffix for all student email is "@students.ccsnh.edu."

Example:	Student Name	James Bond
	Email Prefix	jbond007
	Email Suffix	@students.ccsnh.edu
	Email Address:	jbond007@students.ccsnh.edu

THE BUSINESS PROFESSOR SAYS: Because being in college is like having a job, you should take email etiquette into consideration when sending an email to faculty and staff. Your emails should be: professional, meaning not written in chat speak; with all lower case or upper case lettering (I don't want to feel like you're yelling at me); in complete sentences, so as to show me that you are taking writing seriously; and coherent. If I cannot understand what you are trying to say or asking, it may be difficult for me to respond to your email effectively.

THE ADVISER SAYS: Emails do a really nice job masking emotions and tone. As a practice, if you are upset with something covered in class, a grade you received, a mistake somebody on campus made, or something like that, you should not, repeat should not, send an email when you are angry. Only bad things can come of that, and it would be a lot more effective for you to address an issue you are having in person or over the phone, so nothing gets lost in interpretation. If you need to send an email about something that has upset you, wait until you have cooled off a bit before sending out a very well-crafted, professional email.

Blackboard

NCC uses Blackboard as its online course management tool. All of NCC's online classes run through Blackboard, so if you intend on taking online courses, it is your responsibility to access and fully understand Blackboard's capabilities.

Currently, all instructors are required to make Blackboard available to students and post syllabi there. Most faculty will make your assignments available online as well, and they may use Blackboard for more than just making course content available to you. Some instructors may require you to submit all papers for class on Blackboard through the Digital Dropbox tool, which puts papers through a plagiarism review. They may also require you to participate on a discussion board, which is a class discussion tool. For example, your instructor for Introduction to Sociology may require you to watch a YouTube video and post a "thread," or written comment, on it through the discussion board feature in Blackboard. The discussion board functions like a blog that anybody could contribute to. In addition to this, your instructors may have you take your tests and quizzes on Blackboard.

Blackboard is relatively functional, but there are some things you need to look out for. For instance, you have to make sure that when you submit something through Blackboard (be it a thread for the discussion board, a test, or a paper) that you click the "Submit" button, as opposed to the "Save" button. The two buttons reside close to each other, and it is easy to get confused. If your instructor does not get something you have "submitted" through Blackboard because of your lack of understanding the application, the responsibility falls on you.

THE ADVISER SAYS: You can access Blackboard and student email through "Easy Login." This is designed as a one username, one password tool to access all of NCC's e-resources. You will find your "Easy Login" username and password under the "Personal Information" link in Student Information Systems.

WHERE CAN I GO FOR HELP?

THE ADVISER SAYS: A college or university is technically a community of learners and educators, and it is ESSENTIAL that you start making relationships within the community. This does not involve forming relationships with just your peers, but also with others within the community. Get to know the Registrar, get to know your adviser (strongly encouraged, as this person can advocate for students, and has a beat on what students have contended with since entering into the college), get to know your financial aid officer, get to know college administrators, and, most importantly, get to know your instructors.

THE MATH PROFESSOR SAYS: Students should get to know my name. How else can you discuss the experiences you've had in college?

College is seemingly overwhelming for most new students during the first week of school, with much of that anxiety stemming from not being sure as to what rooms classes are held in. Now that we've moved a day or so into the semester, you are probably becoming accustomed to how this school thing works. With that said, there are some supports available to students that can be really helpful, not only this week but into your college career.

Academic Support Center (Room 100)

Academic supports are located on virtually every campus in North America. This is the place where students find tutoring resources and help with writing and study skills. At larger schools, this may be where mental health counseling and first-year advising is located. This is also where general campus information can be found, like where computer labs are located.

At NCC, the Academic Support Center is located in Room 100 in the Main Academic Building. Within the NCC Academic Support Center is drop-in tutoring, so students can get help with subjects like math, science, computers, and accounting. All drop-in tutoring is staffed by faculty or professional tutors. Students may also apply for peer tutors in Room 100. In addition to this, one of the school's two computer labs is found in Room 100.

Disabilities Services is also located in Room 100. Students who have medical documentation demonstrating a need for course accommodations, such as having more time to finish tests, being able to use calculators on math exams, etc., should visit Room 100 to discuss their situation with the Disabilities Coordinator. It is the responsibility of students with course accommodation plans to give them to their professors during the first week of the semester. Unlike high school, faculty are not made aware of students needing accommodations.

THE 2nd-YEAR COMPUTER SCIENCE STUDENT SAYS: Computer labs are a great place for students who do not have personal computers or access to printers to get their homework done and printed for class. Virtually everything you will write for a course will have to be printed. All computers at NCC are outfitted with Windows 2010 software, and some have Adobe Creative Suite software like Photoshop and Dreamweaver.

THE ENGLISH PROFESSOR SAYS: It is important to have your assignments printed out well before the start of class. I hear a lot of people tell me that they had printer problems, and that accounts for a late submission of work. To me, this is not a valid excuse for late work. Students shouldn't be printing work five minutes before class, and if a student is having a printer issue, it would be good if they access one of the two computer labs at the school, again well in advance of class.

The Business Office

This is the part of the book that is definitely difficult to give perspective on and the most uncomfortable to write about. Obviously school costs money, and schools need to have a mechanism in place to collect money. Schools will have a variety of policies on tuition payments, when they are due, and when a student can get a refund for dropping a class among others. The Business Office is a necessary evil in higher education, and it is something you should work to familiarize yourself with.

This is sometimes referred to as the Cashier or the Bursar's Office at some schools. The primary function of the Business Office is to take payments for tuition, fees, fines, tests, and other costs associated with your education. They also issue and remove account holds, which may prohibit a student from registering for classes or receiving official documents from the school, like official transcripts or proof of enrollment.

Holds are placed on student accounts for a multitude of reasons. From students' failure to complete entrance counseling for financial aid, to them not paying for a campus smoking fine, reasons for holds may be great or small. Primarily, student holds are issued because money is owed on tuition.

> *It is really important to resolve financial balances, as many schools are quicker than businesses in sending outstanding bills to collections.*

In addition to the issues holds can create for registration, financial holds will account for the school not sending your official transcripts to other colleges or employers who request them. If you are planning on transferring, this can hold things up, as the school to which you are planning to transfer cannot evaluate transfer credit until receipt of your transcripts and will, in many cases, not be able to accept you to their college.

THE BURSAR SAYS: Tuition at NCC is always due two weeks before the start of class. You have various options for payment. You could either pay in full, or we offer a payment plan option, which many of you have already signed up for. Otherwise, you would have to have financial aid before the start of the semester. This means that financial aid has to be finalized by this point, that you've signed off on your promissory note, that you've accepted your award. As long as you do this, you will have no problems attending class.

The Business Office is also the keeper of the cost of tuition. If you have questions about how much you will be paying on a semester basis or if there is a possibility for payment plan options, they would be the best point of contact.

At NCC, the Business Office will have information as to when an account paid out, how to access the payment plan option, and whether or not a student has a balance after financial aid has paid out.

Financial Aid Office (Room 097)

> *It is essential that you learn everything you can about the money that will be made available to you through the federal student aid program, through private lenders, and/or through scholarship.*
>
> *It is also essential to know what type of aid you're eligible for, and what it means for you when you leave school.*

This book covers financial aid in more detail in later chapters, as it tends to be a point of confusion for most students, especially new students. Although it is not overly sophisticated in structure, the way it is presented by the government and lending agencies tends to make it seem complicated.

What we'll say here is that apart from accessing and reading the handbook on federal aid the government publishes every year, if you are a recipient of financial aid, you should get to know your financial aid counselor on a working, professional level. This can be one of the most helpful people during your education. If you are not eligible for enough aid to cover your schooling entirely, this person may be able to assist you finding alternative funding sources. By maintaining a relationship with your financial aid counselor and having a working knowledge of what your responsibilities are in the moment and after you leave school, you will have a much better command of your education. You will also avoid that dreaded financial aid curveball that seems to blindside many students every semester (i.e., "you were selected for verification, and you didn't submit the verification form with the appropriate signatures; therefore, your aid has been delayed"—see, hard to really understand what all of that jargon means, isn't it?). This is only one example of many that tends to bite students every fall when they are supposed to be focused on the new school year.

A 2nd-YEAR AUTO STUDENT SAYS: It's really important to pass all of your classes and to avoid withdrawals from class if possible when you receive financial aid. Enough no grades or failing grades can lead to the suspension of your financial aid. And, I don't know about you, but I have to rely on my aid money to be a student right now. It's that important.

The federal government makes FAFSA available to students for a given academic year in January. Students must complete FAFSA for every academic year they are planning on receiving aid. It is essential to understand what semester or term your school designates as the beginning of the academic year.

> *NCC's academic year starts with the summer semester, so if you are planning on taking summer classes and have them covered by financial aid, it is imperative you start FAFSA in January.*

For students planning on being eligible for aid in the fall term, it is preferable to have FAFSA submitted no later than May 1, as this should allow enough processing time ahead of the start of the fall semester.

THE FINANCIAL AID COUNSELOR SAYS: We will request you to complete paperwork to go along with your FAFSA completion. For some, it might be to accept your award and sign your master promissory note, and for others it may be that you've been selected for verification by the federal government. In that situation you would have to provide tax and personal documentation that would confirm that you are indeed the student who has applied for aid. This paperwork should be submitted in a timely fashion when requested. It should also be as complete and accurate as possible, as this will result in a quicker turnaround for financial aid processing.

Financial aid counselors will have direct knowledge as to whether or not you are making the academic progress necessary for continued federal aid, whether or not you are in enough credits to be aid eligible (there is a requirement depending on what you are eligible for), and what you would be eligible for based on the number of credits you are taking, among other things.

To recap, introduce yourself to your financial aid counselor, and get to know this person (and that includes his or her name). This could make a tremendous difference for you moving forward.

Academic Advising Center (Room 099)

A question that comes up often during a student's first year is "Do you know who your academic adviser is?" Many schools are structured without a centralized place to go for academic advising, and some schools require all students to go through an academic advising office.

There is a misperception among many students, faculty, and staff what the role of academic advising is on campuses. Many think that advisers simply choose classes for students, or that their primary role on campus is to assist with the registration process. In most cases, collegiate academic advising has become more about the individual than what classes she takes. Although it is true that advisers assist in the course selection process, they do not prescribe classes. And although they act as a check and balance for students by ensuring that students are not taking classes beyond their majors, the responsibility for scheduling and staying on track for a student meeting goals falls to the student. Advisers assist in identifying student goals, help with the transfer process, assist students in the selection of a major, intervene in academic issues (when required), and advocate for students when the situation warrants it.

At this point, you should have met with your adviser, or a college counselor to select your first semester classes.

THE ADVISER SAYS: It is essential for you to establish a good rapport with your adviser, as, apart from you, he/she will probably have the best knowledge about your academic circumstances and how they relate to your personal circumstances. Although your adviser will not be looking to pry into your personal life, he/she does have an interest in ensuring that your personal responsibilities mesh with your scholastic pursuits.

THE MATH PROFESSOR SAYS: Your adviser will not have access to your grades at any given point of the semester. Your adviser will be able to see all of your final and midterm grades, but rarely do they receive consistent updates from faculty about student performance. You should have an idea about your performance based on whether or not you have been regularly attending class (if you're not, you're probably having performance issues), the evaluated coursework you receive back from your instructors, and if your instructors use the "Grade Center" feature in Blackboard (not all do).

THE ADVISER SAYS: Although it is important to establish a relationship with your adviser, if you feel like you are not being heard, or served best by your adviser, see if you can see someone else. It is essential that you feel comfortable with this person, and there might be some situations where you do not mesh with your adviser. In that situation, it is okay to see someone else. Remember, this is your world, and you make the decisions that best suit your direction.

At NCC, the Academic Advising Center in Room 099 assists most students in selecting classes, but some students are served by the faculty in their department. If it is unclear who your adviser is, now is the optimal time to ask, as faculty and staff are aware of who advises the programs at the school. Your adviser is also listed in SIS under the "Adviser Information" link

Advisers in the Academic Advising Center advise as a team, meaning that if you are in a program assigned to the Academic Advising Center, you can see any adviser in the office. If the person you have seen in the past is not available, you may see another adviser.

THE ADMISSIONS COUNSELOR: The Academic Advising Center is an excellent resource for students looking to transfer. They have a library of transfer information from schools around New England and the country. Every fall, usually in November, the Academic Advising Center hosts a transfer fair, where schools from around the region and into New York State attend, and are there to discuss your future plans, answer any questions, and give you an overall sense if a school will be a good fit for you moving forward.

The Writing Center (Room 100)

Writing is different from Mathematics and Science, as there are no concrete answers that you are seeking, and the writing process is different for everyone. Writing is a creative endeavor, regardless of the type of writing that you are doing. As a writer, it is up to you to craft sentences, paragraphs, and pages of work that consider organization, purpose, voice, and grammar. Therefore, it is theorized that writing is technically never final, and can always change, and getting help with writing is something that writers of all abilities should consider doing since there are no right answers in writing. There is, however, bad writing.

The Writing Center located inside of the Academic Advising Center is staffed by the school's writing faculty. Appointments can be made in 30-minute increments and, during that time, students will sit down for a one-to-one session with a writing professor. It is important to note that you are limited by 30 minutes. You may be able to focus on one thing (i.e., thesis development, organization, readability, grammar) during that time, but you would not be able to focus on all of the things you are maybe looking to have reviewed. The idea of providing this resource is to get your writing to evolve, not to fix your immediate problems. In 30 minutes, you will not go from a draft of a paper, to something polished for submission. Therefore, if you are serious about addressing multiple issues in your writing, you should consider making weekly appointments.

THE WRITING TUTOR SAYS: Unfortunately, the Writing Center is one of the more underutilized resources on NCC's campus. It is, without question, one of the most important resources made available to students. It's free, and you get to sit down with a professor to review your work.

In addition to this, writing tutors will help you develop ideas, but they are not going to help you write your papers. When you write, the words have to come from you. If they are not from you, in your voice, then they are technically plagiarized. Still, the help you will get in understanding how to write, and what works in your papers and does not, is invaluable.

The Writing Center is also a great resource for working on documentation and style for research papers. You may not be required to do many research-based papers this semester, but you will be required to in the future. The tutors in the Writing Center can help you document and properly cite research you pull from the library and other sources, so as to avoid plagiarism.

The Walter R. Peterson and Media Center Library

Although libraries have evolved significantly over the past 10 years, they are terrific places to study, and the Walter Peterson Library at NCC is no exception. It is an extremely quiet place to work and houses one of the two computer labs open to student use on campus. The NCC Library has a professional librarian on staff and several other library assistants to help students with researching and finding the appropriate resources they would need to write their research papers.

The NCC Library has a considerable book collection, with books across many academic subjects. It also has a small DVD and video collection. All book and media resources are available for checkout for all students.

The library really excels in the area of its e-resources. It currently has subscriptions to databases like EBSCOhost and ProQuest, which offer students research opportunities with clicks of a mouse. Students can search for full length news articles, scholarly journals, audio clips, statistics, and ebooks on EBSCOhost and ProQuest in all sorts of academic areas (i.e., history, humanities, nursing, business, etc.). They are as simple to use as Google, and the functionality is the same. The difference is that most of the resources that come up on EBSCOhost and ProQuest are highly credible and can be used in college research. In addition to these online databases, NCC has an e-book collection that contains more than 80,000 titles online.

You should take the time to familiarize yourself with these resources, as you will be using them a lot as you progress through your education. They can be accessed in the library or at home for all NCC students. Remote access to the online resources would require use of your college email username and password.

Chapter 2

Adopting the Creator Role

FOCUS QUESTIONS: What is self-responsibility? Why is it the key to gaining maximum control over the outcomes and experiences of your life?

When psychologist Richard Logan studied people who survived ordeals such as being imprisoned in concentration camps or lost in the frozen Arctic, he found that all of these victors shared a common belief. They saw themselves as personally responsible for the outcomes and experiences of their lives.

Ironically, responsibility has gotten a bad reputation. Some see it as a heavy burden they have to lug through life. Quite the contrary, personal responsibility is the foundation of success because without it, our lives are shaped by forces outside of us. **The essence of personal responsibility is responding wisely to life's opportunities and challenges, rather than waiting passively for luck or other people to make the choices for us.**

Whether your challenge is surviving an Arctic blizzard or excelling in college, accepting personal responsibility moves you into cooperation with yourself and with the world. As long as you resist your role in creating the outcomes and experiences in your life, you will fall far short of your potential.

I first met Deborah when she was a student in my English 101 class. Deborah wanted to be a nurse, but before she could qualify for the nursing program, she had to pass English 101. She was taking the course for the fourth time.

"Your writing shows fine potential," I told Deborah after I had read her first essay. "You'll pass English 101 as soon as you eliminate your grammar problems."

"I know," she said. "That's what my other three instructors said."

"Well, let's make this your last semester in English 101, then. After each essay, make an appointment with me to go over your grammar problems."

"Okay."

"And go to the Writing Lab as often as possible. Start by studying verb tense. Let's eliminate one problem at a time."

"I'll go this afternoon!"

But Deborah never found time: *No, really . . . . I'll go to the lab just as soon as I . . . .*

Deborah scheduled two appointments with me during the semester and missed them both: *I'm so sorry . . . . I'll come to see you just as soon as I . . . .*

To pass English 101 at our college, students must pass one of two essays written at the end of the semester in an exam setting. Each essay, identified by social security number only, is graded by two other instructors. At semester's end, Deborah once again failed English 101. "It isn't fair!" Deborah protested.

Those exam graders expect us to be professional writers. They're keeping me from becoming a nurse!"

I suggested another possibility: "What if *you* are the one keeping you from becoming a nurse?"

Deborah didn't like that idea. She wanted to believe that her problem was "out there." Her only obstacle was *those* teachers. All her disappointments were *their* fault. The exam graders weren't fair. Life wasn't fair! In the face of this injustice, she was helpless.

I reminded Deborah that it was *she* who had not studied her grammar. It was *she* who had not come to conferences. It was *she* who had not accepted personal responsibility for creating her life the way she wanted it.

"Yes, but . . . ." she said.

VICTIMS AND CREATORS

When people keep doing what they've been doing even when it doesn't work, they are acting as **Victims**. When people change their beliefs and behaviors to create the best results they can, they are acting as **Creators**.

When you accept personal responsibility, you believe that you create *everything* in your life. This idea upsets some people. Accidents happen, they say. People treat them badly. Sometimes they really are victims of outside forces.

This claim, of course, is true. At times, we *are* all affected by forces beyond our control. If a hurricane destroys my house, I am a victim (with a small "v"). But if I allow that event to ruin my life, I am a Victim (with a capital "V").

The essential issue is this: Would it improve your life to act *as if* you create all of the joys and sorrows in your life? Answer "YES!" and see that belief improve your life. After all, if you believe that someone or something out there causes all of your problems, then it's up to "them" to change. What a wait that can be! How long, for example, will Deborah have to wait for "those English teachers" to change?

If, however, you accept responsibility for creating your own results, what happens then? You will look for ways to create your desired outcomes and experiences despite obstacles. And if you look, you've just increased your chances of success immeasurably!

The benefits to students of accepting personal responsibility have been demonstrated in various studies. Researchers Robert Vallerand and Robert Bissonette, for example, asked 1,000 first-year college students to complete a questionnaire about why they were attending school. They used the students' answers to assess whether the students were "Origin-like" or "Pawn-like." The researchers defined *Origin-like* students as seeing themselves as the originators of their own behaviors, in other words, Creators. By contrast, Pawn-like students see themselves as mere puppets manipulated by others, in other words, Victims. A year later, the researchers returned to find out what had happened to the 1,000 students. They found that significantly more of the Creator-like students were still enrolled in college than the Victim-like students. If you want to succeed in college (and in life), then being a Creator gives you a big edge.

RESPONSIBILITY AND CHOICE

The key ingredient of personal responsibility is **choice.** Animals respond to a stimulus because of instinct or habit. For humans, however, there is a brief, critical moment of decision available between the stimulus and the response. In this moment, we make the choices—consciously or unconsciously—that influence the outcomes of our lives.

Numerous times each day, you come to a fork in the road and must make a choice. Even not making a choice is a choice. Some choices have a small impact: Shall I get my hair cut today or tomorrow? Some have a huge impact: Shall I stay in college or drop out? The sum of the choices you make from this day forward will create the eventual outcome of your life. The Responsibility Model in Figure 2.1 shows what the moment of choice looks like.

In that brief moment between stimulus and response, we can choose to be a Victim or a Creator. When we respond as a Victim, we complain, blame, make excuses, and repeat ineffective behaviors. When we respond as a Creator, we pause at each decision point and ask, "What are my options, and which option will best help me create my desired outcomes and experiences?"

The difference between responding to life as a Victim or Creator is how we choose to use our energy. When I'm blaming, complaining, and excusing, my efforts cause little or no improvement. Sure, it may feel good in that moment to claim that I'm a poor Victim and "they" are evil persecutors, but my good feelings are fleeting because afterward my problem still exists. By contrast, when I'm seeking solutions and taking actions, my efforts often (though not always) lead to improvements. At critical forks in the road, Victims waste their energy and remain stuck, while Creators use their energy for improving their outcomes and experiences.

But, let's be honest. No one makes Creator choices all of the time. I've never met anyone who did, least of all me. Our inner lives feature a perpetual tug of war between the Creator part of us and the Victim part of us. My own experiences have taught me the following life lesson: The more choices I make as a Creator, the more I improve the quality of my life. That's why I urge you to join me in an effort to choose more often as a Creator. It won't be easy, but it's worth it. You may have to take my word for it right now, but if you experiment with the strategies in this book and continue using the ones that work for you, in a few months you'll see powerful proof in your own life of the value of making Creator choices.

Here's an important choice you can make immediately. Accept, as Creators do, this belief: *I am responsible for creating my life as I want it.* Of course sometimes you won't be able to create the specific outcomes and experiences you want. The reality is that some circumstances will defy even your best efforts. But, believing that you always have a way to

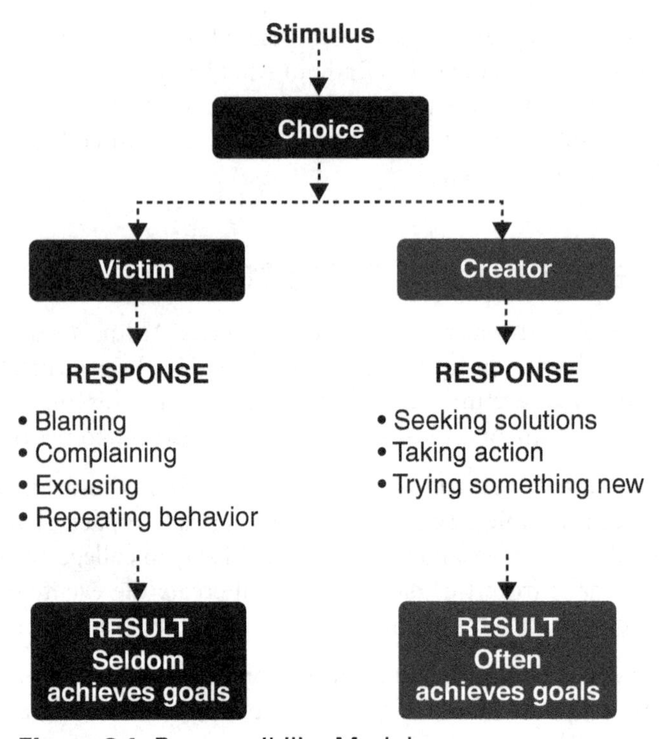

Figure 2.1 Responsibility Model

improve your present situation will motivate you to look for it, and by looking you'll often discover options you would never have found otherwise. For this reason, choosing to accept personal responsibility is the first step toward your success.

Here's a related choice. Set aside any thought that Creator and Victim choices have anything to do with being good or bad, right or wrong, smart or dumb, worthy or unworthy. If you make a Victim choice, you aren't bad, wrong, dumb, or unworthy. For that matter, if you make a Creator choice, you aren't good, right, smart, or worthy. These judgments will merely distract you from the real issue: Are you getting the outcomes and experiences that *you* want in *your* life? If you are, then keep making the same choices because they're working. But, if you're not creating the life you want, then you'd be wise to try something new. We benefit greatly when we shift our energy from defending ourselves from judgments and put it into improving the outcomes and experiences of our lives.

"Oh, I get what you mean!" one of my students once exclaimed as we were exploring this issue of personal responsibility, "You're saying that living my life is like traveling in my car. If I want to get where I want to go, I better be the driver and not a passenger." I appreciate her metaphor because it identifies that personal responsibility is about taking hold of the steering wheel of our lives, about taking control of where we go and how we get there.

Ultimately each of us creates the quality of our life with the wisdom or folly of our choices.

NAME: ______________________ DATE: ______________

JOURNAL ENTRY 1

In this activity, you will experiment with the Creator role. By choosing to take responsibility for your life, you will immediately gain an increased power to achieve your greatest potential.

1. **Write and complete each of the ten sentence stems below.** For example, someone might complete the first sentence stem as follows: If I take full responsibility for all of my actions, *I will accomplish great things.*

    1. If I take full responsibility for all of my actions . . .
    2. If I take full responsibility for all of my thoughts . . .
    3. If I take full responsibility for all of my feelings . . .
    4. If I take full responsibility for my education . . .
    5. If I take full responsibility for my career . . .
    6. If I take full responsibility for my relationships . . .
    7. If I take full responsibility for my health . . .
    8. If I take full responsibility for all that happens to me . . .
    9. When I am acting fully responsible for my life . . .
    10. If I were to create my very best self . . .

2. **Write about what you have learned or relearned in this journal about personal responsibility and how you will use this knowledge to improve your life.** You might begin, *By reading and writing about personal responsibility. I have learned . . .*

ONE STUDENT'S STORY

Brian Moore
Glendale Community College, Arizona

During my first semester in college, I was enrolled in a first-year English class. In high school I was usually able to pull off an A on my honors English papers without much work, and I thought I was a pretty good writer. So when I turned in my first college essay, I was expecting to get an A, or at worst a B. However, I was about to get a rude awakening. When we received our papers back a week later, I was shocked to see a C+ on my paper. I went to the instructor, and she said I just needed more practice and not to worry because I was in the class to learn. However, since I have high expectations for myself, those words weren't very comforting.

About that same time in my Strategies for College Success class, we were assigned to read a chapter in *On Course* about personal responsibility. The main idea is to adopt a "Creator" approach to problems, which I understood to mean basically seek solutions and not dwell on the negative. Then it clicked for me; I am responsible for my grades and I need to do whatever is necessary to get the ones I want. In high school, I could write one draft of an essay, turn it in, and I'd usually get an A, but that approach wasn't working in college. So, now I had to do something different. I started writing my papers before they were due and then meeting with my English teacher at least once a week to get her suggestions. Because I was a full-time student and also worked seventeen to twenty hours a week in the cashier's office, sometimes I had to see her during times that were inconvenient. But I had to be flexible if I wanted her critique. During English class, we do peer editing, and I found that helpful, too. When I was in high school, I only spent about an hour or two writing an essay. Now I was spending at least three to five hours.

To my surprise, after some not-so-great increases in grades, I received what I had been waiting for: my first A on an essay. Although my final grade in English was a B, I learned a number of important lessons. It's really important to take your time with writing, to have your instructor or someone else read a rough draft and give you some suggestions, and then to write a final draft. I also learned that nobody can make the grade for you; you have to be responsible for yourself. I may not always get an A, but I learned to face a challenge, and no matter what grade I receive, knowing that I took responsibility as a "Creator" was the greatest lesson of all.

MASTERING CREATOR LANGUAGE

FOCUS QUESTION: How can you create greater success by changing your vocabulary?

Have you ever noticed that there is almost always a conversation going on in your mind? Inner voices chatter away, offering commentary about you, other people, and the world. This self-talk is important because what you say to yourself determines the choices you make at each fork in the road. Victims typically listen to the voice of their Inner Critic or their Inner Defender.

Self-Talk

THE INNER CRITIC. This is the internal voice that judges us as inadequate *I'm so uncoordinated. I can't do math. I'm not someone she would want to date. I never say the right thing. My ears are too big. I'm a lousy writer.* The Inner Critic blames us for whatever goes wrong in our life: *It's all my fault. I always screw up. I knew I couldn't pass biology. I ruined the project. I ought to be ashamed. I blew it again.* This judgmental inner voice can find fault with anything about us: our appearance, our intellect, our performance, our personality, our abilities, how others see us, and, in severe cases, even our value as a human being: *I'm not good enough. I'm worthless, I don't deserve to live.* (While nearly everyone has a critical inner voice at times, if you often think toxic self-judgments like these last three, don't mess around. Get to your college's counseling office immediately and get help revising these noxious messages so you don't make self-destructive choices.)

Ironically, self-judgments have a positive intention. By criticizing ourselves, we hope to eliminate our flaws and win the approval of others, thus feeling more worthy. Occasionally when we bully ourselves to be perfect, we *do* create a positive outcome, though we make ourselves miserable in the effort. Often, though, self-judgments cause us to give up, as when I tell myself, *I can't pass math,* so I drop the course. What's positive about this? Well, at least I've escaped my problem. Freed from the pressures of passing math, my anxieties float away and I feel better than I have since the semester started. Of course, I still have to pass math to get my degree, so my relief is temporary. The Inner Critic is quite content to trade success in the future for comfort in the present.

Where does an Inner Critic come from? Here's one clue: Have you noticed that its self-criticisms often sound like judgmental adults we have known? It's as if our younger self recorded their judgments and, years later, our Inner Critic replays them over and over. Sometimes you can even trace a self-judgment back to a specific comment that someone made about you years ago. Regardless of its accuracy now, that judgment can affect the choices you make every day.

THE INNER DEFENDER. The flip side of the Inner Critic is the Inner Defender. Instead of judging ourselves, the Inner Defender judges others: *What a boring teacher. My advisor screwed up my financial aid. My roommate made me late to class. No one knows what they're doing around here. It's all **their** fault!* Inner Defenders can find something to grumble about in virtually any situation. Their thoughts and conversations are full of blaming, complaining, accusing, judging, criticizing, and condemning others.

Like Inner Critics, Inner Defenders have a positive intention. They, too, want to protect us from discomfort and anxiety. They do so by blaming our problems on forces that seem beyond our control, such as other people, bad luck, the government, lack of money, uncaring parents, not enough time, or even too much time. My Inner Defender might say, *I can't pass math because my instructor is terrible. She couldn't teach math to Einstein. Besides that, the textbook stinks and the tutors in the math lab are rude and unhelpful. It's obvious this college doesn't really care what happens to its students.* Now I breathe a sigh of relief because I'm covered. If I drop the course, hey, it's not my fault. If I stay in the course and fail, it's not my fault either. And, if I stay in the course and somehow get a passing grade (despite my terrible instructor, lousy textbook, worthless tutors, and uncaring college), well, then I have performed no less than a certified miracle! Regardless of how bad things may get, I can find comfort knowing that at least it's not my fault. It's *their* fault!

And where did this voice come from? Perhaps you've noticed that the Inner Defender's voice sounds suspiciously like our own voice when we were scared and defensive little kids trying to protect ourselves from criticism or punishment by powerful adults. Remember how we'd excuse ourselves from responsibility, shifting the blame for our poor choices onto someone or something else: *It's not my fault. He keeps poking me. My dog ate my homework. What else could I do? I didn't have any choice. My sister broke it. He made me do it. Why does everyone always pick on me? It's all their fault!*

We pay a high price for listening to either our Inner Critic or Inner Defender. By focusing on who's to blame, we distract ourselves from acting on what needs to be done to get back on course. To feel better in the moment, we sabotage creating a better future.

Fortunately, another voice exists within us all.

THE INNER GUIDE. This is the wise inner voice that seeks to make the best of any situation. The Inner Guide knows that judgment doesn't improve difficult situations. So instead, the Inner Guide objectively observes each situation and asks, *Am I on course or off course? If I'm off course, what can I do to get back on course?* Inner Guides tell us the impartial truth (as best they know it at that time), allowing us to be more fully aware of the world around us, other people, and especially ourselves. With this knowledge, we can take actions that will get us back on course.

Some people say, "But my Inner Critic (or Inner Defender) is *right*!" Yes, it's true that the Inner Critic or Inner Defender can be just as "right" as the Inner Guide. Maybe you really are a lousy writer and the tutors in the math lab actually *are* rude and unhelpful. *The difference is that Victims expend all their energy in judging themselves or others, while Creators use their energy to solve the problem.* The voice we choose to occupy our thoughts determines our choices, and our choices determine the outcomes and experiences of our lives. So choose your thoughts carefully.

The Language of Responsibility

Translating Victim statements into the responsible language of Creators moves you from stagnant judgments to dynamic actions. In the following chart, the left-hand column presents the Victim thoughts of a student who is taking a challenging college course. Thinking this way, the student's future in this course is easy to predict . . . and it isn't pretty.

But, if she changes her inner conversation, as shown in the right-hand column, she'll also change her behaviors. She can learn more in the course and increase her likelihood of passing. More important, she can learn to reclaim control of her life from the judgmental, self-sabotaging thoughts of her Inner Critic and Inner Defender.

As you read these translations, notice two qualities that characterize Creator language. First, Creators accept responsibility for their situation. Second, they plan and take actions to improve their situation. So, when you hear ***ownership*** and an ***action plan,*** you know you're talking to a Creator.

Victims Focus on Their Weaknesses
I'm terrible in this subject.

Creators Focus on How to Improve
I find this course challenging, so I'll start a study group and ask more questions in class.

Victims Make Excuses
The instructor is so boring he puts me to sleep.

Creators Seek Solutions
I'm having difficulty staying awake in this class, so I'm going to ask permission to record the lectures. Then I'll listen to them a little at a time and take detailed notes.

Victims Complain
This course is a stupid requirement.

Creators Turn Complaints into Requests
I don't understand why this course is required, so I'm going to ask my instructor to help me see how it will benefit me in the future.

Victims Compare Themselves Unfavorably to Others
I'll never do as well as John; he's a genius.

Creators Seek Help from Those More Skilled
I need help in this course, so I'm going to ask John if he'll help me study for the exams.

Victims Blame
The tests are ridiculous. The professor gave me an "F" on the first one.

Creators Accept Responsibility
I got an "F" on the first test because I didn't read the assignments thoroughly. From now on I'll take detailed notes on everything I read.

Victims See Problems as Permanent
Posting comments on our class's Internet discussion board is impossible. I'll never understand how to do it.

Creators Treat Problems as Temporary
I've been trying to post comments on our class's Internet discussion board without carefully reading the instructor's directions. I'll read the directions again and follow them one step at a time.

Victims Repeat Ineffective Behaviors
Going to the tutoring center is no help. There aren't enough tutors.

Creators Do Something New
I've been going to the tutoring center right after lunch when it's really busy. I'll start going in the morning to see if more tutors are available then.

Victims Try
I'll try to do better.

Creators Do
To do better, I'll do the following: Attend class regularly, take good notes, ask questions in class, start a study group, and make an appointment with the teacher. If all that doesn't work, I'll think of something else.

Victims Predict Defeat and Give Up
I'll probably fail. There's nothing I can do. I can't . . . I have to . . . I should . . . I quit . . .

Creators Think Positively and Look for a Better Choice
I'll find a way. There's always something I can do. I can . . . I choose to . . . I will . . . I'll keep going . . .

When Victims complain, blame, and make excuses, they have little energy left over to solve their problems. As a result, they typically remain stuck where they are, telling their sad story over and over to any poor soul who will listen. (Ever hear of a "pity party"?) In this way, Victims exhaust not only their own energy but often drain the energy of the people around them.

By contrast, Creators use their words and thoughts to improve a bad situation. First, they accept responsibility for creating their present outcomes and experiences, and their words reflect that ownership. Next they plan and take positive actions to improve their lives. In this way, Creators energize themselves and the people around them.

Whenever you feel yourself slipping into Victim language, ask yourself: What do I want in my life—excuses or results? What could I think and say right now that would get me moving toward the outcomes and experiences that I want?

Chapter 3

Debunking the Myths of College

SEEING COLLEGE AS A FRESH START

For new students coming to college for the first time—whether the student is an 18-year-old who recently finished high school, or somebody coming out of the workforce after 20 years—it is easy for them to make the correlation between their success or lack of success in high school and how they are viewed entering college. This is the easiest experience to point to, as it's probably the only experience that would seem to parallel college. We say, it's not that simple.

The message to all students here is this: when you arrive at college, nobody is concerned with your previous academic record and they will not make any assumptions about what your capabilities are based on something that happened in the past. Whether you finished high school or your high school equivalency three months ago or 20 years ago, the makeup of college courses and the social element is entirely different.

You will be sitting in class with peers who are very different from those from previous educational experiences (remember, students are in college because they have chosen to be). You will, in all likelihood, be sitting in classes with instructors who have never met you or experienced your classroom habits firsthand. You will be interacting with staff and administration who may have access to your high school record, but will not base judgment on you and what you may or may not achieve in college.

From this point forward, regardless of your level of achievement in your previous educational situation, what you have done before is irrelevant. Your GPA, your class rank, how you did in Algebra II, how many times you were sent to detention, or if you left high school prior to attaining a diploma does not matter a lick to anyone. All that matters now is that you will be looking to progress through college, that you will do whatever it takes, and that you achieve what you have set out to achieve.

Many types of people with diverse experiences, educational backgrounds, and family circumstances attend college. Many people who attained a Graduation Equivalency Diploma or GED and started in the community college, have moved on to doctoral programs in all fields—Doctors of Medicine, Doctors of Education, Doctors of Philosophy. Many people who are the first to attend college in their family do the same, as do many who grew up in less than ideal socioeconomic circumstances. Even people who graduated bottom of their high school class, barely making it through, start at the community college and move onto advanced degrees. Many people who start out in the most dire of circumstances work their way into dream jobs upon degree completion, and many also write the textbooks that are used in college classrooms around the country.

Regardless of your background, you cannot control the past. It's over and, as a shocker, it will continue to be over forever. If you did very well in high school, great. Nobody can ever take that away from you. It is a tremendous accomplishment. Look to continue that success. And, if you did not perform really well in high school or did not finish, big deal. What you do now is all that matters, and since you are paying for this, college does matter.

UNDERSTANDING HIGH SCHOOL VS. COLLEGE

General Differences

This has been repeated at various times in Chapter 1, and it will continue to be repeated throughout the book, but you are choosing to be in college. Nobody has made this decision for you; there is no law that requires folks in the United States to attend college. Although it might seem as if your parents have decided that you will attend college, you could, in good faith, withdraw from all of your classes tomorrow, and walk out through the front door. Nobody will chase you down and tell you to get back to class.

Not only is college your choice, but it's expensive. Regardless of what kind of college you are at (community, public, private) in what state you are in, college is so expensive that its affordability has become a national question. The vast majority of all undergraduate students in the United States are receiving some kind of aid from the federal government. Close to 89%, in fact, of all full-time undergrads do, with more than half of them receiving loan money as part of their educational funding. These are astounding numbers, considering that less than half of all undergraduate students actually complete their intended degrees or certificates. There is an old saying about college being about experimentation. In many ways this is true, but in looking at cost versus completion, college can be a very expensive experiment.

Compare this with high school, where teenagers up to age 16, in most states, are required to attend. There is no direct cost for public education, other than what comes out of state, local, and property taxes, but students do not pay for classes, they do not pay for textbooks, and lunches even come at a lower price. In high school, all materials short of pens, folders, and paper are issued to students.

In high school and college, the concept of discipline is starkly different. In high school, you are told what to do and how to do it. If you deviate from that, you will be punished with detention or some menial academic endeavor. If you miss class, you could be suspended or held back a year (depending on how much class you actually missed), and three tardies without excuse typically meant that you were on the fast track to detention. So, to recap, discipline in high school relates to corrective measures. You step out of line, there would always be somebody there to ensure that you changed your behavior . . . or else!

In college, the expectation for discipline falls to the student. If you make a decision, all the consequences and rewards for your decisions fall onto your shoulders. This is representative of real life and nobody in college, not faculty, not advisers, and not administrators, is going to remind you to get to class, nor will they take corrective measures to deal with behavioral issues. There is no detention, and there is no obligation to make it to class. The bottom line result for not showing up is failure. The bottom line result of not submitting work is failure. The bottom line result for not considering the quality of work needed to be successful in college is, in most cases, failure. The bottom line result of not behaving appropriately is failure.

Bottom line in college: it is up to you, the student paying for this expensive, invaluable education, to take responsibility for yourself and, most importantly, your success.

High School Faculty vs. College Faculty

Let's clear up what faculty means. Faculty are the people who teach the classes, who are there sharing their experiences, as well as their knowledge of the material. Faculty is a fancier way of saying professor, which of course is a fancier way of saying instructor.

In high school, you called them teachers. You may have had a teacher who had a Master's degree, and, in very rare situations, you may have had somebody with a doctorate. Mostly, however, your teachers had Bachelor's degrees (the very degrees that many of you ultimately want to achieve), and they received training in how to be a teacher as part of their degree completion. That training involved them being a student teacher, and getting supervised classroom teaching experience. Your high school teachers were bound to a curriculum dictated by the state, to ensure that all students were being exposed to the same materials. Without diminishing the role and quality of high school teachers (many of them are terrific in the classroom and they are the ones we remember), but they are given the same direction on discipline, teaching approaches, and conflict resolution, among other things.

College faculty, however, will most likely have advanced degrees or significant practical experience in the field they are teaching in. For people teaching academic classes (as opposed to vocational), it is required that they have an advanced degree (either Master's degrees or doctorates). They are so-called experts in their respective fields, and this, in theory, is what you are paying for. And although a high school teacher gets considerable training on how to teach and manage the classroom, the college professor does not. Professors may get some informal training, but they have to rely heavily on their experiences as students for their method of teaching and course management. They are guided by the curriculum of the school and the classes they teach, not the state. Therefore, there is a little bit of flexibility in teaching what they feel is important.

In high school, teachers most likely checked your work every time you did something. In college, your instructors may opt to not check your work. They may just want to see that you have done it, or they will wait until test time to see to what level you have committed to the material covered in assignments.

Understanding how professors treat assigned work is one of the more difficult adjustments students have when they get to college.

Most college faculty can be very helpful to students, but they are not going to approach students to ensure that all questions are answered about course content. This is up to the student in college, whereas in high school, teachers are constantly monitoring this.

College professors expect you to speak up when you have a question or issue.

In addition to this, your college instructors may lecture as their primary teaching method. In this case, it is up to you to get the material and grind through the class. Not all classes will be as entertaining as this one (wink, wink), and you are expected, as a college student, to be able to listen actively, to take notes effectively, and to study what is covered in class efficiently (this book will address all of these areas).

THE PUBLIC SPEAKING PROFESSOR SAYS: New students oftentimes sit in the back of the class, and think that if they are harder to see then they will not have to contribute to class discussions or ask questions. This is kind of a shame to me because they are afraid of sounding unintelligent to the rest of the class. Speaking up seems to be something they really fear, yet it's going to be something that is expected of them throughout college and into their jobs. I actually find it invigorating when I get students who have experienced college who I had when they first started. They were at once quiet, and after a couple of semesters, they are in the classroom leading discussion. To see them come out of the shell is really great.

Bottom line, faculty expect learning to be initiated and carried out through your approach and commitment to being a student. It is up to you, not them, to ensure that you are getting the course material. Because you were subjected to the opposite approach in your previous educational experience, it may be difficult to completely grasp this in your first year. Your college professors want nothing more than to be effective, but they also want you to be able to take the bull by the horns and create your education.

High School Grades vs. College Grades

There are a couple of things that need to be stated about the differences in grades from high school and college before we get into the nitty-gritty on grades and what they mean. The first is that a student could technically graduate from high school with a D– average. In college, you can expect the minimum institution graduation requirement to be a 2.0 cumulative grade point average (an overall C average). And your degree department's CGPA may be higher than the school's. Also, we see many students asking for extra credit in college, but extra credit has very little bearing on your overall grade. Let's explore why this is.

In high school, you are constantly being evaluated. Your homework is graded, your tests are graded, your in-class participation is graded. The only thing not graded in high school is seemingly your appearance. In a high school class, you may have 10 tests given throughout the year, and although those tests make up a percentage of grades, most or all homework also factors in. So, if a student has graded homework every night in Algebra, then test scores will not factor as heavily into final grades because of all of that homework. This provides high school students a nice buffer for end of semester evaluation.

In college, your final grade may be based on two tests, and your class performance alone. Homework may not factor into your grade at the end of the semester at all. To your professors, you either know the material or you do not, and if you do not, then, in their eyes, you did not take the care to learn the material. Tough. If your grade is calculated based on a midterm and a final, and you do not study effectively on your midterm, then you could be in the land of no return after you get the grade on that test. There is not a lot of room for error in the college classroom. One poor test can put you behind the eight ball.

In high school, As and Bs come a little easier than they do in college. In college, students cannot assume that As just happen because they did the work, showed up to class, or made the effort. C is technically middle ground on the college grading scale, and this is where average begins. The best way to understanding grading and how it is done in most college classes is to consider the following:

- Grades of **A** will be issued for work that not only meets the basic requirements for any given assignment, but exceeds them, in all regards. This work displays excellence in both content and form, and tends to be highly creative, thorough, and thoughtful. It emphasizes a complete mastery of the skills designated for the assignment.
- Grades of **B** will be issued for above average work that exceeds the basic requirements and demonstrates a solid mastery of the skills designated for any given assignment.
- Grades of **C** will be issued for work that meets the basic expectations of any given assignment. The work will exhibit a general understanding of the concepts and technical skills required for an assignment.
- Grades of **D** will be issued for work that meets the minimum standards of an assignment and tends to be extremely deficient in various areas.

The filmmaker Woody Allen famously said that 80% of success is showing up, and that is an adage that holds up in college. If you are not in attendance, then you cannot possibly pass. The other 20% of college is a little more complicated. You are evaluated on getting your work done and submitted on time, but you are also evaluated on your ability to demonstrate knowledge of what you have learned in class. Consider the following questions when you are completing school work:

Does your work go beyond the minimum expectations of the class?
To what level did you go beyond that expectation?

THE COLLEGE COMPOSITION TEACHER SAYS: When writing papers, there are some who believe that the more written, the higher the grade. This is pure myth. In college, if you end up writing a page or two above the page requirements for a paper, you may very well annoy your instructor, who has to spend more time evaluating your work. Discretion is huge in college. Your instructors are simply looking to see if you have a well-supported central idea in your papers. They are not looking for fluff to ensure you get to, or exceed, the page number requirements.

Many college professors will not give out very many As in college, and you should not assume that you should receive an A in a class because you "don't do B, C, or D." With that said, grades do not define the person behind the student, and they should not be worn like Hester Prine wore her scarlet A in Hawthorne's *The Scarlet Letter.* Grades are not representative of self worth. And, although nobody likes to get a C, a D, or even worse yet, it does not mean that the sky is falling if you do. Many academics with fancy advanced degrees will tell you that there were some courses that they took as undergraduates in which they knew they would receive Ds or even (gulp) Fs. They still ended up becoming professional students and are teaching many of the classes you will take. Such grades did not prevent them from achieving a very high level in a university setting.

> *If you want As in college, then you simply have to know what it takes to get them.*

APPROACH

Being evaluated in college is about quality above effort. What this means is that although it is important to make the absolutely highest effort possible, it does not necessarily equate to high achievement. So you need to be prepared to develop and hone an approach to college to help you succeed. Consider the following.

The length of courses is very different from high school to college. In high school, you attended school 181 days per year, at a minimum. This is roughly 36 weeks out of the year, and most classes would run for an entire year. In college, course material is usually covered in 16 weeks, or approximately 20 less weeks than what the run time of a class in high school would be. This is a considerable difference, as students new to college oftentimes struggle with the speed of college classes. In addition to this, some colleges are now offering courses in 8 weeks, four weeks, and an astonishing one week. In condensed classes, 16 weeks' worth of course material is covered in a fraction of the time. This has to challenge your concept of academic commitment, even if that concept was an effective one while you were in high school.

How you approached high school will most likely need altering when you get to college, especially if you had any academic difficulties in high school (either because the material you were subjected to in high school seemed challenging or because you didn't really try). In high school, you were in class roughly six hours per day, and if you are a full-time student in college at 12 credit hours, you are in class about 10 hours per week. Therefore, you have less face time with faculty in college than you did in high school. Looking at this in terms of study time is important. If you aim for the highest grades then, in college, you can expect to put two to three hours of study per credit hour you are taking outside of class. This means that if you are taking a full-time load, 12 credit hours, you can expect to put in between 24 and 36 hours per week in study time outside of class.

In addition to this, your instructors will be expecting you to read and write at the college level, so the expectation in terms of work has increased. You will be expected to write grammatically properly (e.g., no run-on sentences) and to read your work over carefully after completing a writing assignment. Tutoring is something students should seek out as necessary. Take writing for instance. All writers of all competency levels should consider going to get help with their writing, as there is no such thing as the perfect piece of writing. Writing is ever evolving, and students should take this into consideration when they are working on pieces of writing in college.

THE COLLEGE COMPOSITION INSTRUCTOR SAYS: A good practice for working on your writing is to read it out loud, or better yet, have somebody else read your work out loud, exactly as written. This is will allow you to hear the mistakes in your writing.

THE CLASSROOM SETTING IN COLLEGE

One of the major differences between college and high school is the classroom setting. Let's analyze the social side of the classroom setting. In high school, depending on the size of the school, you are in classes with folks who are required to be there, and many of these folks really don't care to be in school. Learning is definitely not the priority (at least yet) in their lives. Many of those folks are in classes with you from your freshman year onward. Although you may make some friends in the process of high school, your peers have a chance to observe you, and make assumptions as to who you are and what you mean in the social context of the classroom. When you get to college, things are entirely different. Few will know you, most will not, and since it is not required, most in college are there to learn and progress toward earning a college credential, not make judgments about you and what you might mean to their lives. They are also there for life experience, and meeting people is part of that. So you may make some friends in the college sphere, but since the college class is short lived (16 weeks maximum), it is difficult for people to have preconceived notions about you, regardless of whether or not you have classes with them in the future. Simply put, whatever greatness or trauma you experienced socially in high school is OVER. Your priority now is to put your best foot forward into something that really counts.

Now to the physical parameters of the college classroom . . . and this depends on the size of college you ultimately attend. In high school, your classes were most likely capped at 35 students (for the giant high schools), although very few ultimately approach that number. In the high school situation, it's easy to get to know your peers and your teachers. Let's contrast this with college. If you have opted to be at a college or university with a large student body, then many of your 100-level and perhaps 200-level courses may cap out from 100 to 400 students. That's right, you may be in a lecture hall with 400 other students learning general Biology. In this situation, it is very difficult to form relationships with your professor or your peers. In smaller institutions, you may not find huge class sizes at the freshman and sophomore levels, but the classes still may be large (35 to 45 students per class), and this still, when most students are new to the environment and being in a classroom with more students than they're accustomed to, can seem daunting or intimidating.

So, we are going to leave it up to you to be proactive. Sit up front, or close to the front. Learn your instructor's name, not just what she looks like. Don't even hesitate to introduce yourself to her. Just walk right up to her after class, and tell her your name and how interested you are in taking on her subject. It's easy. Just right up to her and say, "My name is ________________________________ and I'm really glad to be here." It may be lip service, but it's a good political move on your part, regardless. Your instructor now knows who you are (regardless of how large the class is) and she knows you're proactive and seemingly interested in what she has to present over the semester. Yes. You'll still have to do the work, and a high quality job at that, but since your instructor is a human being (no, faculty have not be replaced by robots ... yet!), there will be a social connection that may benefit you down the road. Also, look in the syllabus for her office hours, which could be a great time for you to get your questions answered one-to-one or even get individualized help with your work.

THE ADVISER SAYS: College instructors will most likely maintain an office hour, at least by appointment. At NCC, most faculty will hold office hours by appointment only, as they are primarily part-time faculty.

MAKING THE RIGHT IMPRESSION

There is an old adage that college is a job, and it's true. It is a job. One that doesn't pay you directly. One that you technically pay for. One that provides you a credential when you have completed the requisite amount of work.

When one walks through the doors to a job on day one, the impression you make right off the bat is something that can carry with you throughout your time on the job. Are you attentive? Do you work hard? Do you have an issue with attendance? Do you play an active role as a participant in meetings? Are you a team player? Do you have the ability to get along with others? Do you understand your role? etc. These are essential questions when employers make evaluations of their employees.

They are also essential questions for you when you walk into the classroom for the first time. Remember, your instructors will form an opinion about you based on your first impression. That's not to suggest that this first impression could have a negative impact on your grade, but as instructors are human beings, it is important to recognize that positive first impressions cannot hurt your overall performance. You may not recognize it now, but there is a political element to being a college student. Let's take the essential questions one at a time,

Are You Attentive?

Do you sit in the front of the room? In the first row? Or are you the person that sits in the back row of the class, the furthest spot from where your instructor will be operating? These all relate to attentiveness because, although you might be paying attention from the back, your instructor would have a harder time seeing your impressive attention span in the back. And although you may have super hearing abilities, as words have to travel through the acoustic spectrum of a classroom, much can be lost in translation when they fall on your ears. This is particularly true in larger classrooms or lecture halls, as many instructors will not be lecturing with a microphone. There is evidence that suggests that sitting closer to the instructor provides students an advantage over those sitting in the back. There's also evidence that suggests the opposite: if a student is a dedicated learner, then they will learn regardless of where they are sitting in the classroom.

One thing is certain, however, the farther away you sit from the instructor, the less likely they will be interacting with you, and with many discussion-based and smaller lecture-based classes, interaction may actually be built into your final grade. Also, depending on where the doors to the classroom are and depending on the size of the room, where you sit may have a relational effect on your attendance in the class. In other words, if it is easy to sneak out of the room, some students may take up the tempting opportunity to leave class. And if you leave class, and it is your responsibility to know what's covered in class, then you are tempting the fates of failure.

Do you look like you are attentively listening? Do you actively take notes? Do you even have a pen in your hand or paper out? These also factor in. One thing is certain about instructors. They go through years of learning, and when they get the opportunity to share what they learn, they love the idea of sharing. They don't, however, love it when students aren't willing to listen to what they bring to the classroom. In fact, they despise it. Regardless of whether or not you are connecting with the content being covered in class, it is up to you to know it. If that means you have to plow through the class to get it, then plow away. It is extremely important to play the role of a student, and that role involves being attentive (just as the role of employee means being attentive).

Beyond this, think of your normal, everyday behaviors. Do you enjoy texting back and forth with your friends throughout the day? Many of you probably do. Do you feel like you're attached to your smart phone? Do you feel that you can't live without Facebook for more than five minutes? Okay. Ten? If the answer is yes, then great. Social media is going to be a very powerful ally to you as a student, and we, as authors, aren't trying to diminish the power of social media. Nor are we the cynical folks who believe that being media literate will be the downfall of a new generation. Quite to the contrary, as you will see later in this book. However, your attentiveness in class cannot be influenced by the accessibility of new media, as tempting as it might be. Because if there's one thing your instructors will hate more than you simply not listening to them, being attached to a media device during class may draw their ire, and think of the political implications of that. You don't want them to know you as the person who's so distracted by their phone that they are unwilling to learn about what's being covered in class. As much as smart phones have revolutionized our society, they present a challenge in the classroom, as their use can give the impression that you are not engaged in class, and if they are used during tests, they can give the impression that your academic integrity is questionable.

Your instructors simply want to see that you are willing to learn, and this starts with being present and attentive, and that you have academic integrity.

Do You Work Hard and Smart?

This is central to being an effective employee and to creating the impression that you are effective in your work. Do you put the requisite time in to get the job done while considering quality? In college, sometimes simply getting the work done is not enough. You have to be willing to commit to working at a higher level, and having an understanding of what quality entails.

For instance, just because you do the Algebra homework assigned every night doesn't mean that you have the knowledge of the math you did to function effectively on the test. This is especially true considering that your instructors may not ask to see your homework, let alone check it to ensure that it's correct. You need to spend additional time to ensure on your own that the homework is correct and then you need to put the study time in to ensure you know how to perform the functions of the math on the test. You not only need to study it once, but you may have to look over it multiple times.

Yes. It is true that not all students are alike. Some students need less time than others to learn material or write a paper, but early on, take nothing for granted. Do not assume that because you didn't need the time in high school to learn the material that it will be the same in college.

Do You Have an Issue with Attendance?

You cannot continually miss work and think the job will be there when you return. This is true no matter how talented you are. The bottom line here is that if you don't go to class you don't pass, no matter how talented you are. In addition to this, your instructor who is forming an opinion of you and, for better or worse, will not see you as being a serious student. Many an A student who had a blip in their educations failed with attendance.

Do You Have to Play a Role as an Active Participant in Class?

Participation accounts for 10% of grades in most classes, and can account for up to 25% of a student's grade in discussion heavy courses. If you are not an active participant in meetings at work it creates the impression that you haven't really thought hard enough about things, that you cannot think well on your feet, or that you are not committed to thinking critically about what's being covered in the meeting. That usually translates into employers thinking you have nothing to contribute to their operations. In the classroom, students who do not play an active role as participants in class are setting themselves up for creating this impression with the instructor, as well. From day one, if you sit close to the instructor, give nonverbal cues that you are receiving the instruction, and provide verbal indication that you are thinking about the material, then the impression you make will be far more considerable than if you don't.

As a challenge, when doing readings or looking over course notes, think of one question, no matter how good or bad in your mind, and ask it during class. It will contribute to a higher understanding of the material and will give your instructor something to hang onto when they are evaluating your contributions to class. Strong participation in a class may account for an entire letter grade.

Are You a Team Player?

This is an odd question when considering college, as you may have heard that it's all about your initiative and persistence, but college will involve working in groups. Whether you go to a school that has a thriving campus life where students are living in on-campus dorm housing, or you go to a commuter college, you will be required to work in groups. The expectation, like if you were working on a team, is that when you are working in a group, you do what you said you were going to do and that you are able to work together. This means that if there are differences in opinion in the group, you may have to mediate those differences. Showing this type of leadership can make a considerable impression. And considering that your instructor may someday be writing a letter of recommendation for you, he/she might be able to attest to your leadership abilities.

Having somebody openly discuss your leadership abilities may lead to a job down the road, or it could help you get into the next college you plan on attending. On the flip side, students who do nothing during group activities and swoop in at the end to collect the grade are ultimately missing an opportunity and creating the impression that they cannot be bothered by such projects.

RECAPPING THE FUNDAMENTAL QUESTIONS TO CONSIDER WHEN APPROACHING THE FIRST SEMESTER

Do you have a full-time course schedule and work more than 25 hours a week at your job?

Are the classes at the times that you learn best?

Are the classes too early in the morning, creating issues of being to class on time or even making it all?

Can you attend tutoring in math?

Can you attend the writing center?

Or does your job get in your way of accessing resources?

If the answer to any of these questions is yes, then is there any way that you can change your current situation?

Additional Questions to Consider

How much time should I put into coursework outside of the classroom?

Do I know the hours to tutoring?

Do I know the hours to the writing center?

Is there any help I can get outside the classroom on my coursework?

Do I know my professors' names?

Are my professors approachable for questions after class?

Do they have an office and office hours? If so, what are they?

Do I know who to go to on campus to have college policy-related questions answered?

Chapter 4

Time Management and Dealing with Procrastination

Time and energy are your most valuable resources.
—Bruce Barbee, Adjunct Professor of Education, UCLA

All of us have the ability to manage our time effectively. However, there is no magic pill that will make you manage your time and stop procrastinating. The reality of time management is that you must want to better your skills.

In order to improve, you must understand that effective time management is the result of numerous choices you make to achieve goals. It's all about priorities. The only way to improve your time management skills is to make better choices. When you think about it, it is impossible to "waste time." Time will continue ticking away no matter what you are doing. You can only spend time inappropriately. Thus, the way in which you spend your time is a conscious choice. For instance, when you watch television instead of studying, you are making the conscious decision that "right now I value television over my academic achievement." Procrastination is nothing more than making a series of decisions that favor postponing something that needs to get done (such as studying) for something else that you would prefer to get done (such as cleaning your room). By assessing the priority of each activity, time management can become a less complex equation. Since time management consists of making good choices, anyone can do it. You just have to be aware of the difference between how you spend your time and how you *want* to spend your time. Effort is still required, but effective management of your time begins with your thought process.

ALIGNING REALITY WITH PRIORITIES

The way you make time management choices depends on your priorities. Since time management is goal-oriented, you need to have a clear understanding of what you want your priorities to be.

While you may think that you have a clear understanding of your own priorities, you must first realize that priorities are determined by how much time they consume. If you spend the most time out of each day watching television, then television is your number-one priority.

Assessment

If Exercise 1 and 2 help you notice that your real priorities do not align with your ideal priorities, then you have just made the first step toward time management: assessment.

When you have a better idea about your priorities, you can make an assessment about your time management. If you are unhappy with your time management skills, there is a strong probability that one of two things is occurring: (1) you have a huge "time-eater" that serves no purpose toward your goals, or (2) you have too much on your plate to possibly perform well in the time allotted.

If you have an activity that hinders your progress toward your long-term goals, then you need to assess the value that activity holds in comparison with your goals. If your "time-eater" is watching television, then you must ask yourself if television is more important than learning and performing well academically.

If you simply have too much on your plate, then you must reexamine your priorities. Often, very high achievers will try to do too much. This could possibly stem from a misconception about being "well-rounded." Most people believe that in order to be well-rounded you have to fully participate in a variety of activities at the same time. Yet, due to time restrictions, chances are you can only participate in a range of activities at a medium quality at best. You simply do not have the time and energy to perform well in everything all the time. A more reasonable and logical view of well-roundedness is: doing one specific activity very well and then moving on to the next activity. Using this definition, you can perform quality work in a diverse range of activities.

Adjustment

Your time management skills will not magically become perfect after just one week. In order to become accomplished at time management, you will need to constantly adjust your schedule to the demands that vary from week to week.

Change occurs in a series of small steps. Patience is the key to adjusting. Significant overall change is made through a number of reasonable or small changes. If the changes you propose to accomplish are too big or drastic, there is a much greater probability that you will not have enough motivation to accomplish them.

MAKING CHOICES

Let's analyze how you make choices, and the refusal to learn from constant mistakes.

Force Field Analysis[1]

Using your assessment, let us analyze how you make decisions that result in behavior. Kurt Lewin created a model for analyzing behavior based on his understanding of physics. Lewin believed that, much like an object's movement, a person's behavior is the direct result of the net forces acting upon that individual. If you hold a pen in the palm of your hand, it remains stable because your arm provides a force holding it up and gravity provides an opposite force holding it down. In order to move an object you can either increase the force on one side or decrease the amount of resistance on the other. When this model is applied to people, you can actually predict what actions and behaviors you will perform. If your positive forces outweigh your negative forces or vice versa, you will most likely act accordingly. For instance, if your motivation to succeed academically is greater than your self-doubt, then your behaviors will reflect this desire to achieve in the form of studying and other methods of preparing for class.

You have both positive and negative, internal and external forces acting upon you at all times. Take a look at this example below. Each arrow represents a force.

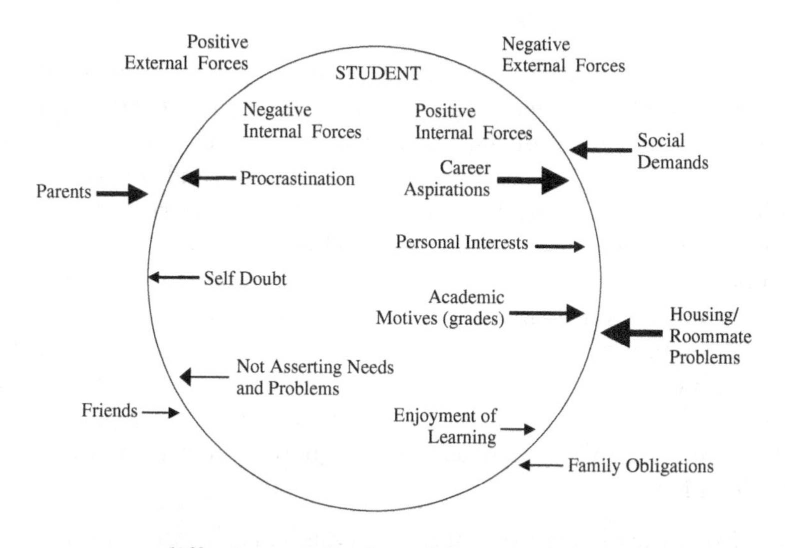

Notice that some arrows differ in magnitude and duration because some forces are greater and last longer than others. As stated at the top of this chapter, time and energy are your most valuable resources. While we have already examined your expenditure of time more closely, it is time to inspect why you make the choices you make.

Your own force field analysis will help you perceive the various forces that supply and demand your energy. Take a few moments to fill in the positive and negative, internal and external forces acting upon your life.

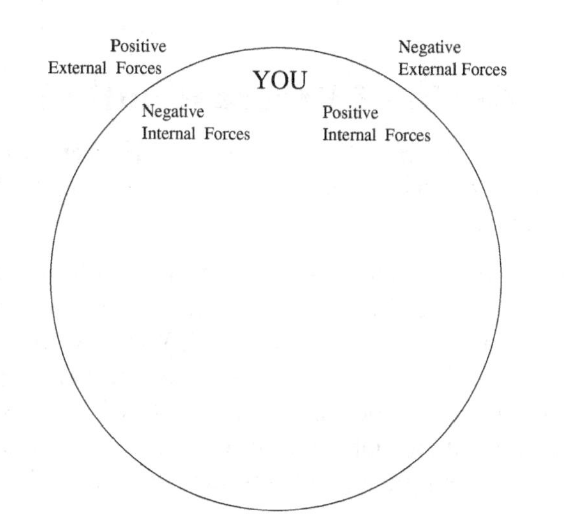

Keep in mind that this model is a snapshot in time. It can be drawn out for a daily basis, for an exact moment in time, or for the purpose of focusing your goals for an entire year. Use this conceptual model to understand that your behaviors are the result of the different forces acting upon you. Notice the role that positive internal forces play. If you are motivated enough, you can overcome any negative forces that might hinder your academic development. Keep in mind that this model helps you predict, analyze, and explain your academic behaviors on a psychological level. You can have all the time in the world, but if you lack energy or motivation, nothing will be accomplished.

A Hidden Curriculum[2]

Let's be realistic. A good deal of time management issues arise from simply not having enough time to study all the material that professors assign. It is nearly impossible for any college student to complete all of the assigned work for each class in the time allotted. Thus, students find it hard to accomplish the unrealistic "formal curriculum" assigned by instructors. The formal curriculum of teachers is all of the work assigned to a student, including class, reading, writing, and other work. However, as you probably know by now, it is nearly impossible for any one student to meet all of these expectations. Students often feel that most professors on their campus don't understand that they have other classes that demand their attention as well. Consequently, students constantly assess the hidden curriculum of each course. As previously mentioned, the "hidden curriculum" of a course answers the question: "What do I really have to do in order to obtain a good grade?" (Note well: The objective of the hidden curriculum is a good grade, which does not necessarily translate into learning.)

Once students assess the hidden curriculum for a class, they institute *selective negligence*. In other words, they purposely don't study portions of the formal curriculum in order to save time and energy for other classes or activities. In college, most selective negligence will appear in the form of skipping or skimming reading assignments deemed superfluous.

Discovering the hidden curriculum of any class can be a useful tool to aid your time management and progress. However, beware of abusing the hidden curriculum (e.g., missing a lecture or discussion, neglecting too much reading, etc.). Too much selective negligence will only result in a lack of knowledge and experience coupled with mediocre grades at best.

Breaking the Cycle of Procrastination

Everyone procrastinates from time to time; it's part of life. Yet, making a habit of procrastination will have adverse effects on your studies. We are trying to discover a way to break this cycle of unproductive behavior.

Alcoholics Anonymous defines madness as doing the same thing over and over while expecting a different result each time. If you continually procrastinate and expect a different result each time, then you are not being logical. You probably tell yourself "This time will be different because {______}." Yet, if there is no extra effort placed into the activity to differentiate it from the rest of the failures, the result will be the same. Without learning from your mistakes, you will inevitably repeat them. It's the same as trying to make better cookies while using the exact same ingredients and procedures. Something must change.

A simple yet effective method for breaking your habit is: don't do it. If you know it will only end up in failure, why bother procrastinating? It is similar to the old anecdote: A man goes to see his doctor and says "Whenever I do this, it hurts." The doctor tells him, "Don't do that."

GETTING THINGS DONE

Of course, telling yourself to "not do that" is a lot easier said than done. The following are some effective methods that will motivate your progress.

Set Manageable Goals

Setting goals is probably the best way to motivate yourself. First, set some long-term goals that you want to achieve in life, in college, and in this quarter/semester. By writing down your goals you can help reevaluate your value system. Assessing your values will consequently affect your priorities.

Next, for each day or study period you should have an intermediate goal that can be reasonably achieved. Do not tell yourself, "I'm going to read *Crime and Punishment* today," because it is simply unreasonable. Instead, set a more reasonable goal with the time allotted, such as "I will read at *least* two chapters before I hang out with my friends."

Use Socially Distributed Willpower[3]

Often, it is difficult to even muster up the motivation to study in the first place. In order to counteract this idleness, you can use your peers to increase your willpower. By setting up study groups or weekly meetings with peers, you increase your motivation through social interaction. When two or more people are involved, you feel more committed to the task your group is involved with because your peers hold expectations of you. You have willpower distributed by social interactions and expectations. Make a pact with your friends that you will study with them on a weekly basis on the same day and time. Aside from your peers, you can also set appointments with your professor or teaching assistant to help motivate your progress.

Try Chunking Your Tasks

Often, big tasks can be daunting and overwhelming to focus on; this results in procrastination. Let's use an analogy to discover a great method of managing big tasks. Pretend for a moment that you have a dead elephant stuck in your room. You don't know how it got there; but it smells horrible; and you need to remove it. Unfortunately, the dead elephant won't fit through the door. How do you get it out? Simple: cut it up into manageable pieces that will fit through your doorway.

In this analogy, the dead elephant represents a horribly daunting task and the doorway is symbolic of your "doorway" of allotted time. If you have a 20-page paper due at the end of the term, "chunk the paper" into manageable parts. Ten two-page papers is a lot more manageable than one 20-page paper.

Aside from this gruesome analogy, Einstein had his own way of looking at impossible problems. When questioned about how he had proved such mind-bending theories in physics, Einstein said that he didn't see it as one big impossible problem, but many smaller, solvable problems. Notice that he didn't try to remove the problem altogether but simply perceived it differently. Breaking down a daunting task into smaller tasks is an effective way to succeed in a timely manner.

Be Flexible

Since you will have to be making constant adjustments to your schedule, you will have to be flexible in your expectations. Things won't always go as planned, so expect the unexpected. You can plan ahead for unexpected events by scheduling "time buffers" in between activities. Also, one way to help minimize surprises is to allow more time for a task than you think you will need.

Use Inertia

As Newton said, an object in motion stays in motion. The inertia of studying will keep you going, but getting started is the hardest part. Force yourself to start studying for at least 10 minutes; chances are you will keep it up.

Know Yourself

Be honest while planning your schedule. Do not try to make too many drastic changes too soon. Change is a gradual process. By being realistic and honest, you minimize the discouragement caused by failing to meet idealized expectations. Be sure to base your changes upon your personal assessment of your priorities. High achievers have the tendency to know themselves, understand their capabilities, and think realistically.

Know your peak times to achieve during the day. If you find you study best at night, then do so. Also, keep in mind that other distractions may interfere with your peak times, such as running into friends on campus during the daytime. Schedule the time to perform important tasks during your peak-energy times.

GENERAL TIPS FOR TIME MANAGEMENT

- *Get organized.* The most common way to keep track of things is a day planner.
- *Make sure you get a planner that fits your lifestyle.* You should be able to carry your planner with you anywhere, so make sure it suits you. Even though a planner might be "top of the line," it won't do you any good if you never use it.
- *Try to write everything down in your planner.* When you first begin using one, refer back to the lists you made with your commitments ranked according to priority. Go through your class syllabi at the beginning of the term and write all the reading assignments, exams, papers, etc. in your planner. This way, you get an accurate idea of how to budget your time for the rest of the term and minimize the need for cramming.

- *Be focused.* Concentrate on one activity at a time. Make sure you have the pertinent information before you start a task.
- *Don't be a perfectionist.* Trying to be a perfect person sets you up for defeat. Nobody can be perfect. Difficult tasks usually result in avoidance and procrastination. You need to set achievable goals, but they should also be challenging. Striving for greatness is good; striving for perfection is simply unrealistic.
- *Learn to say no.* For example, an acquaintance of yours would like you to see a movie with him tonight. You made social plans for tomorrow with your friends and tonight you were going to study. You really are not interested. You want to say no, but you hate turning people down. Politely saying no should become a habit. Saying no frees up time for the things that are most important.
- *Daily Lists.* One of the most effective ways of being productive everyday is to make "to-do" a list. The list should be prepared in the morning or early on in the day. Every time you get something done, check it off the list. Checking off items will motivate you to get another task accomplished.
- *Combine several activities.* Another suggestion is to combine several activities into one time block. While commuting to school, listen to taped notes. This allows up to an hour or two a day of good study review. While showering, make a mental list of the things that need to be done. When you watch a sitcom, laugh as you pay your bills. These are just suggestions of what you can do to combine your tasks; but there are many others. Above all, be creative, and see what works for you.
- *Take care of yourself.* Schedule daily time to exercise, relax, meditate, spend time with friends, sleep, and eat a nutritious diet. Avoid overly stressing out your body with incessant working and studying. Many students overwork themselves through cramming, resulting in exhaustion and burnout. By planning carefully and working in small increments, you will stay healthier both physically and mentally.
- *Keep the important stuff in mind.* Remind yourself, "There is always enough time for the important things." If it is important, you should be able to make time to do it. Examine and revise your time goals on a monthly basis and be sure to include progress toward those goals on a daily basis. Put up reminders in your room about your goals.
- *Make and keep deadlines.* Be sure to set deadlines for yourself whenever possible. Reward yourself when you meet those deadlines, especially the important ones. If you finish an essay early, treat yourself to a movie or call up that friend who was waiting for you to finish studying. Balance is crucial.

SUMMARY

Your time management skills and ability to eliminate procrastination derive from your decision making. Every second of every day, you make choices. Right now, you are making the choice to read this chapter instead of doing something else. By being cognizant of this decision-making process, it will be easier for you to motivate yourself to devote the necessary time and energy to your studies.

NOTES

1. Edward C. Anderson, "Forces Influencing Student Persistence and Achievement," *Journal of Counseling Psychology* 32, no. 1 (1982): 94–103.
2. Benson R. Snyder, *The Hidden Curriculum* (Cambridge: MIT Press, 1973).
3. Daniel Fessler, "Windfall and Socially Distributed Willpower: The Psychocultural Dynamics of Rotating Savings and Credit Associations in a Bengkulu Village," *Ethos* 30 1/2 (2002): 25–48.

BIBLIOGRAPHY

Anderson, Edward C. "Forces Influencing Student Persistence and Achievement." *Journal of Counseling Psychology* 32, no. 1 (1982): 94–103.

Dyer, Wayne. *The Sky's the Limit.* New York: Simon & Schuster, 1980.

Fessler, Daniel. "Windfall and Socially Distributed Willpower: The Psychocultural Dynamics of Rotating Savings and Credit Associations in a Bengkulu village." *Ethos* 30 1/2 (2002): 25–48.

Lewin, Kurt. "Group Decision and Social Change." In *Readings in Social Psychology, ed.* T.M. Newcomb, E.L. Hartley et al. New York: Holt, 1947.

NAME: ______________________________ **DATE:** ____________________

JOURNAL QUESTIONS

Do your ideal priorities match with your real priorities? How are they the same? How are they different?

What is a hidden curriculum and how can you utilize it?

How do people convince themselves that procrastination is acceptable?

List three things you can do to increase the efficiency of your time management and reduce the frequency of procrastination.

List three ways you can motivate yourself to use a planner.

NAME: ______________________________ DATE: ____________________

EXERCISE 1.

Write down your ideal top five priorities for your average academic week in the spaces below.

Priorities

1.

2.

3.

4.

5.

These are your idealized priorities. In essence, you have just written down how you want to spend your time. To help you better visualize this, look at how you actually spend your time by filling in this weekly time grid according to the past week. Remember to include social activities, grooming, and commuting in addition to academic commitments.

WEEKLY TIME GRID

	SUNDAY	MONDAY	TUESDAY	WEDNESDAY	THURSDAY	FRIDAY	SATURDAY
5 am							
6 am							
7 am							
8 am							
9 am							
10 am							
11 am							
12 pm							
1 pm							
2 pm							
3 pm							
4 pm							
5 pm							
6 pm							
7 pm							
8 pm							
9 pm							
10 pm							
11 pm							
12 am							
1 am							
2 am							
3 am							
4 am							

NAME: ______________________________ DATE: ____________________

EXERCISE 2.

Find out the top five time consumers in your week (excluding sleep) and enter them into the spaces below.

Real Priorities

1.

2.

3.

4.

5.

To what degree are your idealized priorities the same as your real priorities? Are there any surprising time consumers in your life?

In the space below, write down all the things you accomplished in the last 72 hours.

____

____

____

____

____

Now, make a list of all the things you should have done.

____

____

____

____

____

How do these two lists compare? How does this reflect upon your priorities? Decide right now if you want to do something about any discrepancies between your ideal life's schedule and your current life's schedule.

Chapter 5

How to Study

CASE STUDY

Yasmine

Yasmine is hoping to get into the nursing program; however, the prerequisites include several difficult science courses. This semester she is taking general biology, and everyone in her class is majoring in some area of allied health. She needs to start working on a research assignment, but she has never been to her college's Learning Resource Center/ Library and doesn't know how to begin. She's tried a Google search for her topic but isn't sure she is finding the kind of scientific articles her teacher expects the class to use as sources.

On her last sociology test, Yasmine did not do as well as she had hoped. When she read the textbook the first time, she started at the beginning of the chapter and read straight through. The material was difficult to understand, so she used her highlighter to help keep her focused. When it came time to review for the test, though, there was so much highlighted material it seemed like she was reading the whole chapter over again. Her notes were not much help either, as she could not seem to tell what was important. She tried to write down everything, but couldn't keep up with the lecture and missed critical data. Even though she spent a lot of time studying, she felt like nothing she thought was important was on the test.

Reflections

- What are some of the common study problems Yasmine experienced?
- How could the SQ4R method help Yasmine study more effectively?
- What does she need to know about using resources in the Learning Resource Center/ Library?

INTRODUCTION

Many college students are working while attending classes, and finding enough time to study seems to be a problem for most of these students. The recommended study ratio for college courses is a minimum of two hours outside of class for every hour in class. When questioned about how much time they spend studying, students generally admit that their study time is much less than this recommendation. This chapter will teach you several strategies to help maximize your study efforts so that you use the time you have to the best advantage. Textbook study strategies covered in this chapter include:

- *Making Sense of a Paragraph*
- *Marking Your Textbook*
- *SQ4R System*
- *Charting*
- *Specialized Study Techniques*

We'll also look at ways to improve your ability to concentrate so that your study sessions will produce effective results. Topics in the "Making the Most of Your Study Time" section include:

- *Recognizing and Coping with Distractions*
- *Focusing your Attention*
- *Creating a Productive Study Environment*

Finally, we'll take a look at the academic resources available to today's college students and encourage you to check out the academic support services available on your own campus.

Pretest

Directions: Check "Yes" or "No" to identify areas where your study habits could use improvement and to demonstrate your familiarity with academic support services available on your campus

	Yes	No
1. I always look through my textbook before the class starts to see what the course will cover.	____	____
2. I usually look up unfamiliar words when I'm reading my textbook, using the text glossary whenever possible.	____	____
3. I highlight/underline my textbook and make margin notes when reading.	____	____
4. I am able to pick out the topic sentence in a paragraph.	____	____
5. I have a regular place for studying, and my study environment is free from distractions.	____	____
6. I plan my study sessions when I know I am rested and will be able to concentrate.	____	____
7. Before starting to read a new chapter, I look over headings, illustrations, and chapter questions so that I have a general idea of the topics to be covered in the chapter.	____	____

8. If I have several chapters to read, I divide the material into several reading sessions.
9. I set specific goals for each study session (number of pages to be read, draft of English assignment to be completed, reviewing for a test, etc.)
10. I study new material as soon as possible after class.
11. Before studying new material, I take a few minutes to review the previous assignment.
12. I reread highlighted, underlined, and/or boldfaced material and any margin notes I've made when I'm reviewing for a test.
13. I am able to predict questions that are likely to be on the test.
14. I try to find a study partner for each course.
15. I know where the reference and periodicals sections are located in my campus Library/Learning Resource Center.
16. I know where the "open" computer labs are on my campus.
17. I already know how to use the Internet.
18. I have already used one of the campus tutoring services.

If you checked "No" to five or more statements, this chapter is especially for you! Textbook reading and study strategies can make a big difference in your reading comprehension skills. In addition, using the academic support services available on your campus can greatly increase your chances for academic success.

TEXTBOOK STUDY STRATEGIES

Making Sense of a Paragraph

Many of you will be taking a college reading course in which you will develop reading comprehension skills through a series of vocabulary and textbook reading exercises. We won't attempt to cover that same material but believe it is useful for you to understand the paragraph structure, as most textbook material and other reading assignments are constructed in a series of paragraphs.

The typical paragraph contains a topic sentence stating the author's major point. Often it is the first sentence in the paragraph, but not always. The body of the paragraph consists of one or more sentences providing supporting detail, and the conclusion restates the main idea or serves as a transition to the next paragraph.

Let's look at a paragraph from a college catalog discussing the Illinois Articulation Initiative:

> Transferring to another institution is a complex process. In order to understand the process of course transferability, students should use two sources of data.

Topic Sentence: States the main idea.

> First, students should consult the www.itransfer.org website for specific information about the General Education Core requirements and certain academic majors. Second, students should meet with a counselor or advisor to seek information on how courses will be used when transferring to another institution. Once a student narrows down the choices of transfer institutions, she/he should consider how well his/her selected courses fit the requirements of the four-year college. While the approved IAI General Education Core Curriculum allows for completion of the transfer institution's lower level general education requirements, there are specific course selections in general education, the major, and electives, which can enhance the transfer process.

Body of sentences to support the main idea.

Conclusion: Supports the point that course transfer is a complex process.

Not all paragraphs will contain a clearly stated topic sentence. Some may use a series of supporting sentences that lead to a conclusion. Try to identify topic sentences or main ideas as you read, and pay special attention to any conclusions drawn by the author. When reading critically, try to identify whether the supporting detail provides facts or just the author's opinion. Try to restate the author's main idea in your own words.

Marking Your Textbook

Once you've learned to identify the main idea, search out details, and look for the author's conclusion, you can use those skills to highlight important points in the textbook and to make margin notes for review use. What should you highlight? Concentrate on the following:

- Identify the main idea and important supporting details
- Definitions and key terms
- Names and dates if significant to the passage (history texts, for example)
- Answer the "Big 6" from your reading: **Who? What? When? Where? Why? and How?**

Let's take a look at a reading passage with highlighted text and margin notes.

European Multicultural Foundation

Europe is home to many ethnic groups—some long established, some of recent introduction—with a wide range of cultures and traditions. There is no dominant nationality, language, or culture.

Europe: No dominant nationality or culture.

Most people, whatever their background, are strongly attached to their own language and customs. Many people may feel threatened by the rapid changes and shifting values of present day Europe. The anxieties of settled communities and the difficulties experienced by more recent arrivals are two sides of the same coin.

Cultural anxieties.

To attempt to force people into a common mold, either with an individual country or across the continent is undesirable and contrary to the aims of the European Union. A more positive approach accepts cultural differences as valuable in themselves. Only if we learn to appreciate each other's way of life with all our differences and similarities will intolerance become inconceivable. This rich diversity is Europe's greatest strength.

Europe's Greatest Strength: Cultural diversity.

The European Multicultural Foundation was established to promote mutual understanding and respect for the customs and cultures of others, thereby ensuring the development of a successful civil society. The foundation's aim is to sponsor projects across boundary lines that will help build a Europe in which all people, whatever their origin, can live peaceably together.

EMF: Goal is peaceful co-existence based on mutual understanding and respect.

Remember Yasmine from our case study? Don't fall into the trap of highlighting too much information. When done properly, reading the highlighted text portions and margin notes as you're reviewing for a test and comparing the text information with your class notes become powerful study techniques.

The SQ4R System

The SQ4R reading-study system is a widely used study system. While this system is time-consuming, it forces you to be very involved with the text. If you have difficulty reading and understanding even ten pages of a text at one time, this system of reading can be particularly helpful. The five steps identified below are comprehensive but easy to remember:

S = **Survey** your reading assignments to get a general overview of the topic to be covered. What looks familiar? Has the instructor covered this in class? Pay particular attention if the author has used an introduction or list of objectives to be covered in a chapter. Look at discussion or study questions and at the summary at the end of the chapter. They will help you to focus on what the author considers important.

Q = **Question.** Turn the chapter and unit headings into questions and then read to answer the questions. Use the "Big 6" mentioned earlier—Who? What? When? Where? Why? and How?—to formulate your questions. Write your questions down as you survey the chapter. After reading each section, see how readily you can answer them.

R1 = **Read** to answer the questions you've developed. Find one or more main idea and supporting details. Make margin notes. Pay attention to graphs, charts, and illustrations as you read. If you have the time, fold your paper in half vertically and put the questions on one side and the answers on the other side. In this way you can quickly review as needed. If you know you won't take the time to write out the questions and answers, concentrate on jotting down your questions as margin notes and highlight the material that answers them.

R2 = **Recall or recite.** Reciting material to yourself out loud helps you to absorb the information. This step is especially helpful with definitions, with date/event pairings, and with material that needs to be memorized. It's also a good idea to pause every 5–10 minutes (or after every section of text) and try to recall what you've already covered by reciting aloud or by jotting down the main ideas.

R3 = **(W)Rite** the answers to your questions in the form of notes or journal entries. Writing engages multiple senses and helps you remember the material.

R4 = **Review,** review, review! Every review session helps you retain the information for an upcoming test. Make sure your test review includes rereading your highlighted text and your classroom notes.

Charting

Once you have read the textbook material and have taken notes in class, how can you best organize the material for review and later test preparation? Using "Information Charts" is a powerful technique. Charting allows you to *compare and contrast* several topics, events, or people in relation to specific criteria or questions. For example, in every recent U.S.

presidential election, the two major candidates were likely to be compared on some of the following issues:

ISSUES	REPUBLICAN	DEMOCRAT
Economic issues—taxes, foreign trade, employment levels, space research . . .		
Defense and safety issues—$$ for military, disaster funding, federal and state law enforcement . . .		
Personal priority issues—gun control, abortion, social security, disease research, health care . . .		
Leadership and character issues—family values, morality . . .		

If you were to complete the chart above with specific information you've gathered about each candidate, you would have a start toward making an informed choice about the candidate for whom you will vote. You can use this same technique in a literature class by comparing and contrasting how various authors/poets used sensory imagery in their writing. In an introductory psychology class you can compare and contrast psychoanalytic theories, or compare strengths and weaknesses of various Civil War generals for a history class. Combining your answers to the questions you've generated when reading and the notes you've taken in class into this highly usable form can save you lots of time in test preparation.

SPECIALIZED STUDY TECHNIQUES

Studying Literature

Most of you will be taking an English class in which you will be asked to read novels, plays, poetry, and essays. The four main components of fiction are: *character, plot, time and place, style and tone.* By focusing on these characteristics for each reading assignment, you will be able to increase your understanding of a novel, short story, play, etc.

- *Character:* Who is the central character in the story? How does this character react to the problems she/he faces? What circumstances caused him/her to respond in the way she/he did? If the character takes stupid actions, how would you advise him/her to handle the situation differently? Do you like this character—why or why not? Can you identify with the main character? If yes, how or why? If no, why not? Be aware of your reactions to the character as you read and try to predict how you think she/he will handle upcoming situations.
- *Plot:* As you read, try to anticipate what will happen next. Where is the author heading with the story? Why? What circumstances are revealed that motivate the characters to action/inaction? How will the story end? Would the ending have been different if the main character(s) had reacted in another way?
- *Time and Place:* In what time period and in what environment does the story take place? Why do you think the author chose this setting and time period? Do the prob-

lems or difficulties experienced by the characters seem trivial in today's world, or are they problems that seemingly transcend time? How does the setting affect the story—would people in different parts of the world feel the same way about the conflict presented? Would the story be likely to end in a different way if the setting and time period were different? Do you feel a connection to the time and setting used by the author—why or why not?

- *Style and Tone:* The writer's style is what makes his/her writing identifiable. The use of descriptions and dialogue, the amount of explanation or background she/he supplies about why the characters act in the way they do, and the sentence and paragraph structure used determine a writer's style. The tone is established by the emotions and feelings expressed in the writing. As you read, think about the author's style. Are there passages you feel like reading over again? Are there passages that you really dislike? What emotions do you experience—sadness, happiness, loneliness, etc.? Are you more aware of the language used or the way the author makes you feel? You may wish to write down specific passages that illustrate the author's style so you can quote them in an essay, term paper, or critique.

Being aware of these four characteristics of writing while you read your literature assignments will help you understand what the author is trying to communicate. Using the charting technique will help you organize and process the information.

Studying Science

Most of you will be taking at least one science or mathematics course, and those of you planning to transfer will need to take both a biological and a physical science. Physical sciences like chemistry and physics require you to learn problem-solving techniques and how to apply those techniques to sample problems.

- Work through sample problems in each section before moving on to the next section.
- Once you have completed a sample problem in the text satisfactorily, check for a similar problem on which to practice. Reinforce the technique you have learned.
- Biology requires that you understand key concepts and how they relate to important processes—the digestive, reproductive, and circulatory systems, for example. "What," "How," and "Why" questions are especially important in biology.
- Science classes will make extensive use of diagrams, maps, and charts. Make sure you understand the information presented in these illustrations.

Studying the Social Sciences

If you are working toward an associate degree, you'll have to complete one or more social science courses. Frequent choices are economics, history, psychology, and sociology.

- Surveying the chapter is especially important in the social sciences. Get an idea of the topics you'll be covering before you start.
- Don't try to read the entire chapter at once. Focus on the first topic, generate questions from the chapter headings, and read specifically to answer those questions.

- Use the questions at the end of the chapter to further direct your reading.
- "What," "Why," and "How" questions are especially important in the social sciences.

Studying Mathematics

Many of you will have to take several mathematics courses to complete your desired degree. Learning algebra seems particularly difficult for some students. Using some of the following techniques should be helpful.

- Work through the first example in the chapter. After completing this problem successfully, work similar problems in the "Exercises" section to reinforce the concept.
- Translate algebra, a new (maybe even foreign) language for some of you, into English (or your native language). Practice saying out loud what the problem means and what you're being asked to do.
- Find the section in your text that talks about the "rules" of algebra. For example, *the order of adding two or more numbers* ($6 + 5 = 11$ and $5 + 6 = 11$) *does not change the sum.*
- Remember that *mathematics is a sequential and cumulative process*—you must do the homework daily, and you must practice each new type of problem. You can't afford to "skip over" concepts you don't understand. Learning the foundations and mastering each step is essential for later success.

Studying Foreign Languages

Mastering a foreign language obviously requires a significant amount of memorization. Oral drills with a classmate are especially useful. Use every opportunity to practice—listen to conversations around you or to television programs in the language you are studying. Practice, practice, practice!

MAKING THE MOST OF YOUR STUDY TIME

A common complaint of college students is, "I just can't seem to remember what I've read!" Students swear that they've spent hours reading the text but simply can't remember the content. Look over the list below and see how many of the statements describe what happens when you try to study.

- Noise, interruptions, or uncomfortable temperatures really bother me when I'm trying to concentrate on my assignments.
- Between school, work, and my other responsibilities, I'm usually just too tired to concentrate when I sit down to do my homework.
- I find it really difficult to get back on task if someone interrupts me when I'm studying.
- Just starting a long or difficult assignment often seems overwhelming; I don't know where to begin.
- I do read the text material, but I don't always understand what I've read.
- If I have something on my mind, I just can't concentrate on my homework.

Do these statements sound familiar? If you recognize yourself, then you need to pay attention to the strategies and techniques that follow.

Recognizing and Coping with Distractions

Internal and external distractions can seriously interfere with your ability to concentrate when you study. Some major distractions include:

- *Stress:* Worrying about a disagreement with a family member, friend, or co-worker; feeling pressure from a coach or boss to "produce"; being concerned over a family member's illness; or worrying about paying bills are ways in which you can be distracted from studying.
- *Physical Discomfort:* Anytime you feel physically uncomfortable, you're likely to be easily distracted from trying to study or from paying attention in class. If you normally eat breakfast and don't have time to eat before leaving for class, you're likely to be more focused on getting food than on paying attention to the lecture. If you didn't have enough sleep the previous night, it will be difficult to pay attention when you sit down to study. If you are trying to study in the Learning Resource Center/Library and the temperature is too hot or too cold, you may need to get a sweater or even move to another area. Pay attention to your physical needs! If you can change the situation by getting something to eat or changing your study location, do it. If you're really too tired to study, go to bed and get a fresh start in the morning. The important thing is to change your environment when you can so the time you spend studying will be productive.
- *Lack of Motivation:* If you don't see a connection between your courses and your career and life goals, you may find it difficult to concentrate on lectures or studying the text. If you are a culinary arts major who hated high school English, you may find it really difficult to spend the time and effort necessary to do well in a required communications/writing class. You may, however, have to pass one of these courses to graduate, even though you may not see how you would use English writing skills on the job.

  The English instructor has students from many, many career or major areas and doesn't have the option of personalizing the curriculum to fit the individual interests of each student. If you find yourself in this kind of situation, you have to take a long-range viewpoint. You don't have to like all of your courses, but if they are degree requirements, you have to pass them to graduate. This approach is also necessary if you haven't decided upon a major and are simply completing general education requirements. You may hate the thought of taking a speech course, but this is a requirement you'll have to meet.

  Investigate all of your options before scheduling classes for each semester. What general education requirements do you have remaining? If you need 3 additional credits in the social science area, look over your choices. What social science courses did you enjoy in high school? Talk to other students, and see what they're taking. Popular favorites are psychology and sociology, but these may not appeal to you. Maybe you'd rather try anthropology or a political science course.

- *Daydreaming:* Letting your mind wander can thoroughly derail a study session. You may not even realize it is happening until time has passed without getting anything accomplished. There is so much going on in our lives that we often don't reserve "down time" to process all of the issues facing us. Our study session might be the only time we sit down quietly to think. All of a sudden random thoughts intrude into our minds. Thinking about recent events, what we need to do tomorrow, the next date, what to wear, what's happening this weekend, what's on television tonight, and a host of other things crowd out the subject matter we're trying to learn.
- *Interruptions:* Have you ever been all set for a badly needed study session and had a roommate barge in on you? How about a telephone call from a friend who just wants to chat? This is a situation in which you'll need to use assertive communication skills.

  Your study time is important, and you need to be sure that your interruptions are kept to a minimum. If you find that your study time at home is a series of interruptions, you will need to consider studying on campus or at your local library. Next semester, try scheduling one or more breaks between classes to use for study time on campus.

Creating a Productive Study Environment

Where and how you choose to study is a personal preference. Many students feel the need to have absolute quiet in their study area, while others insist they can't study without music. Some students like to study with classmates, while others prefer to study alone. By now you've probably established a study pattern, but all study habits can be improved. Consider these points as you evaluate your own study habits:

- *Study Location*—In general, having a designated study area helps to put you in the "study mode." You may prefer a desk in your bedroom, the Learning Resource Center/Library on campus, or the kitchen table. The location you choose should be as free from distractions and/or interruptions as possible.
- *Study Conditions*—Overhead lighting or a lamp with good diffused lighting is important. It's ideal to have a desk or table with ample writing area, plenty of space for books, and a supportive chair. If you have a computer, make sure you still have enough writing space. If you're studying in the Learning Resource Center/Library, the natural light plus overhead lighting creates a fine atmosphere for most people.
- *Organizing Your Supplies*—If you're primarily studying at home, it's easy to organize your study supplies. A bulletin board or corkboard is useful for posting weekly assignments, due-dates of major projects, and other schedule reminders. Pens, pencils, markers, and highlighters can be kept in a pencil bag or small plastic box if you don't have a desk drawer to hold these items. Larger supplies like folders, notebooks, paper supplies, and reference materials can be kept in a plastic or cardboard box if necessary. If you tend to study on campus or in another location, a briefcase or backpack can be fitted with your basic study materials. Be sure to have a dictionary within reach!

Focusing Your Attention

With the work schedule and outside responsibilities you have, it is important that you accomplish as much as you can in each study session. All study sessions are not created equal! Use the following strategies to make the time you spend pay off.

- *Set a specific goal for each study session.* What do you need to accomplish? Do you have 30 math problems to do, 50 pages of history to read, and need to draft a paragraph for English? Look over each assignment and be clear about the requirements. At the end of your study session, check your progress. Did you allow enough time to finish one task? If not, plan extra time for your next assignment of that type.
- *Break large assignments into smaller parts.* If the assignment is to read three chapters for psychology by the end of next week, target one chapter for each of three study sessions between now and then.
- *Identify and use your peak energy times for study.* Study for your most difficult classes during the early morning hours if your energy level is high in the morning and decreases as the day moves along. If you are a "night owl" and really feel energized during the evening hours, use that time for study. Your ability to get the most from any study session is definitely affected by energy levels.
- *Combine mental and physical functioning.* Some textbook reading can be boring. Try to keep actively involved in the process by using the study techniques previously discussed. Jot down specific questions, and read to answer those questions. Make margin notes. Compare lecture notes to the text. Be an active participant in the study process!
- *Start with your most difficult study task.* If mathematics is easier than English, start with your writing assignments first, and get them out of the way. Your math problems can then be tackled after finishing the most difficult task, and you will feel good about having had a productive study session.
- *Try using a study partner, but have some "ground rules."* Many new students like to plan their schedules so they are taking courses with one or more friends. If you plan to study together, remember that each study session should be devoted to a specific goal. Make plans to review certain chapters, quiz one another in preparation for the test, etc. Don't just plan to get together to study without a specific task in mind; it is too easy to have this kind of study session end up with nothing getting accomplished.
- *Use study breaks.* After 1–1½ hours of study, take a short break. Taking 5–10 minutes to stretch, move around, or get a drink helps you to focus again with a higher level of concentration. Remember, it's how you spend the time that counts!

USING ACADEMIC SUPPORT SERVICES

Guidelines for Using Tutoring and Other Support Services

One characteristic of the academically successful student is his/her willingness to seek support services when needed. Most colleges have a variety of academic support services, and it is advantageous to use these services on a regular basis. Students frequently don't think about getting help until they are seriously behind or really having difficulty in keeping up with the course work. Don't let this happen to you. If you wait to get help, the most convenient tutoring times may already be booked, or you may not be able to make a comeback because you've fallen too far behind. The following guidelines will help you make the most of the campus tutoring services:

- *Attend class regularly!* If you've missed a class, you're already behind.
- *Be prepared!* If you're having difficulty with a specific type of math problem, try to work it out to the best of your ability. Take your work to the tutoring session so the tutor can see where you got off track.
- *Understand the difference between your tutor and your instructor!* It is not the tutor's job to re-teach the information that was already presented in class.
- *Don't expect the tutor to do the work for you!* If you need help with a writing assignment for English class, take in your rough draft. The tutor can work with you on identifying grammar problems but will not correct the work for you.
- *Make an appointment!* Help may not be available on a "drop-in" or emergency basis. Many students wait until mid-term to get help, but by that time in the semester the tutors are already heavily booked. It's better to start going for help as soon as possible—even for only one or two questions. Once you've finished the tutoring session, schedule your next appointment to make sure time will be available.
- *Keep your appointment once you've made it!* Making a tutoring appointment and then not showing up denies another student the opportunity to get help. Please be considerate of your tutor and of other students' needs. If you are ill or know that you won't be able to keep an appointment, please call the tutoring service to let them know and to reschedule your appointment.
- *Be realistic about how much help you can receive!* Some students seem to think that they're entitled to tutoring services on a daily basis. Realistically, this isn't going to happen—generally once or twice a week in each subject area is all that will be available. Check with the program providing the service to make sure about tutoring limits.

Using the Learning Resource Center/Library

The first step is to learn about the Learning Resource Center/Library resources by walking around and identifying the main sections or areas. Most college libraries contain three major areas:

- ***The Reference Section*** is where dictionaries, encyclopedias, and other specialized reference works that cannot be checked out of the Learning Resource Center/Library are located. All reference materials are coded with an "R" to indicate that they are non-circulating material.
- ***The Stacks*** are the groups of books that you can check out. This is generally the largest area in the library. Most of the resources you will use are found in this area. This section is organized by subject area, using the Dewey Decimal System of classification. For example, 300–399 includes social science areas such as psychology, sociology, anthropology, etc. Literature is found between 800–899. Works of fiction are classified alphabetically according to the author's last name. Large signs identifying the numbering system are normally posted at the beginning of each row. Some libraries use the Library of Congress system.
- ***The Periodicals Section*** stores newspapers, journals, and magazines that are published on a daily, weekly, monthly, or quarterly basis. However, to find articles on a particular subject, you will want to search the library's online databases. Most libraries subscribe to a number of databases that include the complete texts of thousands of magazine, journal, and newspaper articles.

Everyone knows what a newspaper is, but not everyone is aware of the differences between a magazine and a journal. Table 1 identifies a few distinctions between the two, but not every magazine or journal will have all of these characteristics.

Never hesitate to ask a librarian if you need assistance in finding information, locating materials in the Learning Resource Center/Library or using the computer databases. Most college libraries have reference librarians (trained information specialists) who can help you navigate your search for materials in the library and online.

Library Databases

A database is an organized collection of information. Most college libraries can generally be accessed through an online catalog. You can search the catalog by author, title, subject, or keyword.

College libraries also have a number of commercial databases for which they pay a subscription charge. These databases provide access to magazine, journal, and newspaper articles, and even to some radio and television transcripts. You can search these subscription databases from any computer on your campus by going to the library's Web page and clicking on a command similar to "Start your search for books, articles." Most databases also have off-campus access, but you may need to get a password from the library staff.

Tips for Searching Databases

When you're looking for information in a database, it's a good idea to study the screen to see the various search features and note how they are arranged in that specific database. You will find that most databases follow the example of Internet search engines and will automatically put you in a basic keyword search.

A keyword search is when the computer program scans items in the database for the words you type in the box. If you're looking for magazine or journal articles on adopting children, and type "adoption" as your keyword, the computer will look for any article that includes the word adoption in the title, abstract, or text of the article. As you can imagine, this could bring up articles that have little or nothing to do with adopting children.

Keyword searching is helpful for more specific inquiries. If you were looking for information on an adoption case involving a child known as "Baby Richard," you would have much quicker results trying a keyword search of "adoption" and "Baby Richard" than in scanning all the articles under the subject of adoption.

When you're looking for a broad topic such as adoption of children, it is often better to do a subject search. Many databases provide a "subject" or "topic browsing" option. This differs from keyword searching in that someone has actually looked at the material and decided to what subject area or category to assign it. So, when you do a subject or topic search in a database on "adoption," any materials you retrieve should actually be about adopting children.

Databases provide a number of ways to make your inquiry even more specific. Many databases give you an advanced or customized search option. This allows you to combine different types of searches such as adding keywords to a subject search. Most databases also give you "limit" options. You can usually limit your search to full-text (meaning the com-

Table 1

MAGAZINES	JOURNALS
Aimed at a general audience. Readers may not have any specialized knowledge of the topics.	Aimed at a specialized audience. Readers may be professionals or scholars in a certain field.
Avoids technical language so that the general public will understand the material.	Technical language is used because the intended audience will understand it.
Usually no references to other sources are provided.	References to other articles or books are provided. (Bibliography)
Generally the articles are informative or entertaining. Takes a popular approach.	Articles may be research reports or case studies and are academic or scholarly in nature.
Mass advertising. Advertises products that appeal to a wide audience. Example: toothpaste	Limited advertising. Advertises specialized products that are used by technicians or professionals. Example: scientific equipment

EXAMPLES OF MAGAZINES	EXAMPLES OF JOURNALS
• Ladies Home Journal • National Geographic • People • Reader's Digest • Sports Illustrated • U.S. News and World Report	• Families in Society • JAMA (Journal of the American Medical Association) • Journal of Marriage and the Family • Journal of Social Issues

plete text of the article). You can also limit by date and by the title of the newspaper, magazine, or journal. Many academic databases let you limit your search to "peer reviewed" or "refereed" journal articles, which are more scholarly in nature because they have been reviewed by professionals in the field. If you need a scholarly journal article, using this "peer reviewed" limit would kick out popular magazines such as *People* or *Newsweek*.

Not all databases are the same. You will notice that CQResearcher specializes in political and social issues. For general searching, a database like InfoTrac, FirstSearch, or EBSCO would be useful.

Most databases have a print command somewhere on the screen. This feature reformats the article into a "printer friendly" (text only) version. Before you print, go to "print preview" (on the toolbar) to see how long the article is and how it will look. Print only the pages you need. If you are being charged per page to print, you may prefer to send the article to your e-mail or save it on a disk or jump drive.

Another tip for online searching is to use the "find" command on your computer's toolbar as a shortcut. When you pull up the article, go to "edit" on your toolbar and then select "find." Type your keyword(s) in the box. When you click "find," you will go directly to those words within the text of the article.

Using the Internet as a Research Tool

The Internet is a tremendous source of information. However, you must be careful to evaluate any material you find on the Web. The books or articles that are in the library's databases have already gone through an evaluation process before being published. That's not true of the Internet where anyone can put anything they want on a Web site.

As you use the Internet, pay particular attention to the **URL** (the Web site's address). The address always ends with the "domain" of the site. The Internet is divided into domains such as .com for commercial sites, .gov for government sites, and **.org** for organizational sites. An educational or government site is apt to be a reputable source of information. Of

The following list is a sample of databases that may be available on your campus:

Magazine and Journal Articles

- CQ Researcher (current social and political issues)
- Full Text Electronic Journal Holdings List
- EBSCO (for any subject plus specialized databases on business and health)
- E-Subscribe (ERIC education documents)—generally campus-based access only
- InfoTrac (for any subject and specialized business databases)
- FirstSearch (for any subject plus specialized databases such as ABI Inform for business and Medline for health)
- Illinois Periodicals Online (full text of some Illinois magazines)
- Lexis-Nexis Academic Universe (business, legal, medical, and news)
- Literature Online Reference (literary criticism)
- Matter-of-Fact Database (statistics)
- Proquest (criminal justice)

Newspaper Articles

- EPSCO Newspaper Source
- Historical New York Times
- Newsbank
- Lexis-Nexis News

course, you can find useful material in other domain sites. When doing an evaluation of information found on the Web, you will need to ask yourself some questions.

- First, who is responsible for the Web site?
- Is there information on the author or organization that created the site?
- Does the person or organization have credentials or expertise in the subject presented on the Web site?
- Is there any possible bias by the author of the site? For example, an advocacy organization may be taking a particular position on an issue. While this doesn't mean the information they present is incorrect, you should be aware that they might be presenting their position in a more favorable light.
- If factual information is presented on a Web site, is there any documentation or sources listed to corroborate the facts?
- And, finally, how up-to-date is the information?
- Always be sure that your instructor allows the use of Web sites for your research.

You access the Internet through a "search engine." A search engine is a computer program for locating information on the Web. The Internet has thousands of search engines available. Some are commercial search engines like **Google** (www.google.com) or **Yahoo** (www.yahoo.com), while others such as the Librarians Index to the Internet (www.lii.org) are developed by groups or nonprofit organizations.

While search engines operate in a similar manner to database searching, they do vary. Some use quotation marks or + and – signs to search for a phrase or to add/block terms from an inquiry. Use the help screens for tips and examples when searching.

"Advanced" or "guided" search screen options let you:

- Search for an exact phrase
- Add or subtract key words
- Limit search by language
- Limit search by date posted on the Web site or last time updated
- Limit search by where the key words are in the document (in the title, in the text . . .). Key words in the title are more likely to give you useful sites for your topic.
- Limit search by domain (area). For example, if you are looking for a statistic, you could limit your search by .gov (government) Web sites.

Many search engines provide directories that allow you to click on a particular subject listing and bring up Web sites on that subject. Directory searching can be useful when looking for information on a broad topic.

Remember that one of the keys for successful research is to **start locating information as soon as possible**. Get acquainted with your topic by reading a summary in an encyclopedia. There are even specialized subject encyclopedias for condensed information. As you become more familiar with your topic, you can narrow the subject, do a more thorough search, and be certain your sources are credible.

SUMMARY

In this chapter you were introduced to several study systems. You also learned about barriers to concentration, how to focus your attention on your studies, and how to create a productive study environment. We've also encouraged you to use the academic support services available on your campus, especially tutoring services and your campus library/Learning Resource Center. Remember that good study habits and the strategic use of academic support services make the difference between "getting by" and academic success.

NAME: ______________________________ **DATE:** ____________________

JOURNAL QUESTIONS

Although Yasmine studied for a long time, her study habits were not that effective. Describe some changes that she could make to be more productive.

Analyze your current study habits and study area.

- Describe your positive study habits—what are you doing right?
- List some ways to improve your study time.
- Describe your typical study area.
- Tell why it works/doesn't work for you.
- If you need to make changes in your study areas, what changes will you make?
- Which strategies from this chapter will you use to increase your concentration?

NAME: ______________________________ DATE: ____________________

EXERCISE 1.

Use the SQ4R study system to create a study guide for this chapter. Survey the chapter and turn the chapter headings into questions. Your answers to the questions will form an outline to use when reviewing for the chapter quiz.

1. Name of textbook ______________________________

2. Name of chapter ______________________________

3. Read the introduction. Briefly state what you are expected to learn in this chapter.

   ____

   ____

4. What new terms or vocabulary words are in this chapter?

   ____

   ____

   ____

5. On the following page, fill in the chart **completely** by taking each heading and major subheading in the chapter and writing a question that will be answered in that section of text. After you have read the chapter, go back and answer your questions. An example is done for you showing two possible questions from the heading *Marking Your Textbook.*

HEADING	QUESTION	ANSWER
Marking Your Textbook	What should I mark in my textbook? or How do I know what to mark in my textbook?	Main ideas with supporting details or Answer the big 6 from the reading: who, what, when, where, how, and why

Chapter 6

Study Skills and Strategies

Give a man a fish and you will feed him for a day. Teach a man how to fish and you will feed him for a lifetime.

—Ancient Proverb

This chapter will focus on building personalized study behaviors that will enhance your academic performance.

PART I: ESSENTIAL ELEMENTS FOR ALL LEARNERS

There are certain fundamental behaviors that are essential to academic success. While some of these behaviors might seem obvious, they are absolutely vital to achieving high grades in a competitive environment. Often, most students suffer from a gap between "knowing" these obvious behaviors and actually doing them.

The Importance of Effort

You will have to put forth more effort in a university; it is significantly harder than high school. As a result, you must put forth more effort in comparison to your previous academic endeavors.

Universities select students primarily based upon test scores and grades, thus placing you among your intellectual peers. While you may have been able to slide by high school on intelligence alone, you will find that this approach will not work at the university level. In order to distinguish yourself from your classmates you will simply have to study harder and learn more. Effort is the key factor in determining academic success. In an environment of intellectual equals, instructors award the best grades to the students who put forth the most effort. Exams, discussions, and coursework are all specifically designed to show how much effort you have exerted, not merely how smart you are.

Quality of Effort[1]

In each activity of your life, you determine the quality of the effort that you put forth. Studying and participating in class are no different. Let's take the example of the lecture. A very low quality of effort might include physically showing up for class, but sleeping through the lecture. A slightly higher quality of effort would be attending class and jotting down a few notes. An even higher quality of effort would be sitting in one of the first three rows, taking precise notes, paying close attention, and participating in the lecture by answering or asking questions.

Please be sure to note the difference between *quantity* of effort and *quality* of effort. Students commonly underachieve because they mistake a high number of hours spent studying for effective studying. Much like the maxim "work smarter, not harder," quality of effort specifically refers to the effectiveness of the effort, not necessarily the amount. To use a specific example, a student might spend hours upon hours reading and studying course material. However, if this time is used poorly by neglecting to read well and learning only through repetition, then the student has put forth a low quality of effort. Students that put forth a high quality of effort must use effective reading, listening, learning, and studying techniques in order to increase the efficiency of their effort.

The level of your physical and psychological involvement will directly impact your achievement. The students who achieve the highest grades put forth a high quality of effort. Not only do they typically exert more effort toward class; the *quality* of their effort is superior. In addition, the number of students performing at this high level is smaller.

A's are not received easily in college; they are earned. The well-known guideline of academic effort is two hours of studying for every one hour of class per week. For instance, if you attend a lecture four hours a week for a certain class, then it is *expected* that you study at least eight hours a week for that same class. Students who perform at high levels of achievement know that there is no excuse for not studying. They know that in order to obtain the grade they desire, they must put in the necessary effort.

The Hidden Curriculum: Realigning Expectations

Since you only have a finite amount of time and energy, the quality of your effort will vary from class to class and week to week. In order to be as successful as possible, you must maintain realistic expectations of the work required of you. Each class brings new challenges that require adaptation. You will constantly have to readjust to different expectations of workload, teaching style, testing methods, and subject matter (among other obstacles). Therefore, understanding the goals of your professor is vital to assessing the quality of effort you will need to expend. In other words, determining the "hidden curriculum"[2] of each of your classes is crucial to gauging your quality of effort. Talk with students who have already taken the class. Consult any reviews about the class that may be posted online. Professors' office hours are a great opportunity to clarify the main goals of the course, the expectations of classroom participation, or the requirements for assignments. While it might be surprising, teachers are very willing to share their expectations with their students. Instructors know that clear expectations will enhance student learning and completion of class assignments. Putting forth the effort to understand your professor's expectations will save you a lot of time, energy, and frustration down the line when it comes time to study for exams, write papers, or complete projects.

Active Learning Techniques

The more active you are in a task the greater your comprehension. As the levels of learning progress, each subsequent stage is more involved than the last. Gaining an understanding of the different levels of learning is the first step toward achieving more effective study habits. Developing actual behaviors that utilize higher levels of learning will further enhance your comprehension of class material.

Active learning tasks require greater expenditure of time and energy than other tasks, but they pay off in the long run. Take a look at the following learning pyramid displaying effectiveness of various learning strategies.[3]

The strategies outlined in the pyramid increase in effectiveness as the base broadens. Notice that the tasks that require small amounts of time and energy are the least effective, while the tasks that ask the most of you will aid in your efforts to retain information and learn deeply. Also, take note that in college, students primarily receive the most amount of information from lectures (the category that aids least in retention of material). Thus, you must view lectures as the beginning of the learning process, not an end within themselves.

Attendance at lectures should be considered mandatory because the majority of examination material is mentioned during lectures. However, merely attending a lecture will not serve your best interests with regard to learning. Other methods must be employed in connection to or during a lecture.

Completion of assigned reading, much like the lecture, is essential to your understanding of class material and preparation for examinations.

Combining modes of learning is a form of enhanced learning. Study that involves auditory, visual, and kinesthetic activities will serve to increase attention, comprehension, and retention.

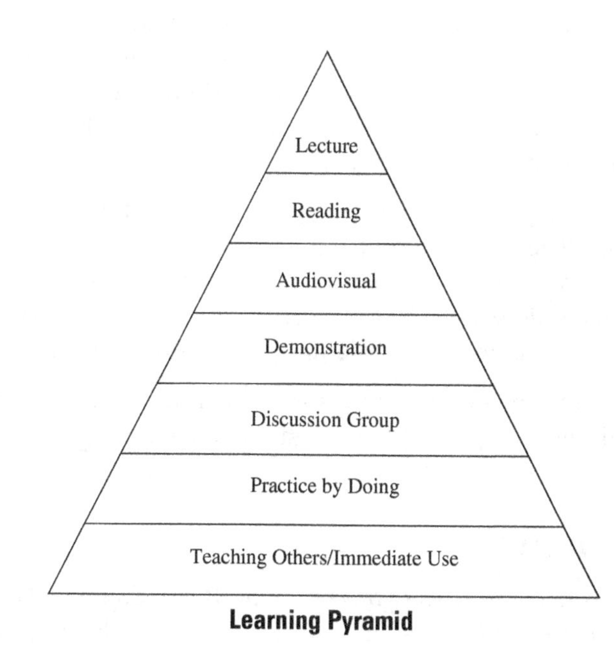

Learning Pyramid

Finding methods of demonstrating your knowledge (either through experimentation or self-testing) will increase your ability to retain information due to their active qualities.

Much like the lecture, attending discussion is mandatory for students who are serious about achieving academically. In fact, discussion is an active task that combines all three modes of learning and typically delves deeper into the coursework by exploring high levels of learning. Furthermore, regular participation in discussion is a great way for your teaching assistant to recognize your effort and potentially boost your grade accordingly.

The act of practicing by doing is highly interrelated with discussing and teaching. Find ways that you can assert your knowledge of a subject by actually performing tasks that require a deeper understanding of the material. Such strategies might include writing and problem solving.

Finally, the task of teaching is the best way to learn material for numerous reasons. If you can teach the material to someone, then it proves that you have knowledge of the material. Also, teaching often requires you to explain the material in many different ways (since we all learn differently), thus deepening your comprehension of the material. In addition, teaching requires the use of all three modes of learning and promotes a deeper understanding of the material. Finally, being able to teach someone else tests your mastery of the material; in a lot of ways, testing in the university is essentially the demonstration of your ability to teach the material back to the professor.

Office Hours

Office hours are blocks of open time that professors and teaching assistants set aside each week for students to ask questions and discuss material, and they are beneficial in a number of ways. For one thing, office hours are a chance to review and deep process the material through intellectual dialogue. Having a discussion with your professor allows you the opportunity to ask questions as well as receive feedback. Introduce yourself in the lecture and let the professor learn your name. Then attend office hours with a specific question or point of discussion. You can clarify a topic or ask how the professor thinks about the subject in order to better understand it yourself. Do not think that office hours are reserved for emergencies only. Professors and graduate teaching assistants hold office hours to field all sorts of questions, comments, and concerns.

Another great benefit of getting to know your professor is that it will motivate you to pay more attention in class. The more you get to know your professor as a person, the more you will become interested in the material discussed in the lecture. Furthermore, when you avail yourself of office hours professors get to know you and recognize the effort you are exerting, which could make a big difference for borderline grades and letters of recommendation.

Yet, students are still intimidated by professors. This fear is unfounded. The difference between high school and college is that in high school, teachers talk to you; in college, teachers talk *with* you.

Study Environment

Your environment strongly influences your behavior. If you do not believe this, try shouting the next time you are in a library—it is quite difficult. Studying in the right environment will help you to be an active learner with your material. In general, a good study environment contains the following qualities:

- **The environment is set aside for the specific task of studying.** In most cases, your room is not a good place to study for this reason. Since you use the room for multiple tasks, it contains great potential for distractions. Students living in the dorms or apartments have everything they could possibly need in their room within reach at all times. Avoiding distractions is essential for forming an environment that is conducive to focusing. Also, if a place is used for a specialized reason, it is harder for you to utilize the room in another way. For instance, what do you do in the gym? You have only one option: work out. Find an environment to study in that will restrict your behavior to the task you want to accomplish. In addition, surrounding yourself with others doing the same task will motivate you even further.
- **The environment *displaces* you from distractions.** By physically displacing yourself, you are less likely to end your study session too quickly. If your room is distracting, then find a place to study that takes a couple of minutes to reach. If you walk 10 minutes to the library, then you will be more likely to stay longer since it takes time and energy to get there and back. Displacement is similar to taking several hours to reach a vacation spot. Since it takes a long time to get there, you will not want to leave too quickly.
- **The environment fits your noise level preference.** Some people like absolute silence while others prefer a little background noise. Also, while studying with music in the background might be acceptable for some types of learning, studying with the television on is never a good idea.
- **The environment has a cool room temperature.** A cool room temperature will increase your body's ability to focus. Scientifically speaking, it is easier for the human body to stay awake and concentrate in a cooler environment. Ideally, it should be on the cool side, not too cold. Avoid stuffy or hot environments that will make you want to sleep.
- **The environment allows and encourages good body posture.** If your environment determines your behavior, then your posture determines your focus. Sitting with better posture will improve your body's ability to stay awake. Over the course of your life, your body has become accustomed to certain positions or moods that would put it to sleep. Basically, the more comfortable you are, the easier it will be to fall asleep. This is why studying on a bed hardly ever works. Good sitting posture consists of placing your backside at the back of the chair while aligning your spinal column with the back of the chair as well. Keep your chin up and avoid slouching. If you find yourself dozing in class or while studying, try correcting your body posture and wait a minute or two (it will not help you focus instantly). If your body posture looks like you are focusing, it will be a lot easier for your mind to do the same.
- **The environment has ideal lighting for studying, called diffused lighting.** Just about any classroom, study lounge, or library will have diffused lighting. Diffused lighting has multiple light sources in the room (preferably overhead) and none of them are overpowering. Usually, a good way to see if a particular lamp is too overpowering is to hold up your hand about a foot off the desk. If you can see very

clearly defined fingers and a dark shadow (e.g., the shadow the sun casts), the light is too bright. Ideally, your hand's shadow should be thin and difficult to distinguish. Too much, or too bright lighting is bad because the light will reflect off the paper, blinding your eyes. Excessive light actually makes it harder for your eyes to focus on the reading.

Seek out the best places to study on and around your college campus. Typically, libraries on campus will provide you with the best facilities for studying.

Effective Study Blocks

Research indicates that taking regular breaks increases learning performance.[4] When study blocks are spaced apart (called distributed practice), they are more effective than longer, clumped blocks (called massed practice). In addition, during distributed study blocks, the learner's performance will gradually improve until a peak level is reached. With the addition of regular breaks, the learner's performance will tend to surpass the previously established peak. In general, research shows that learners who take breaks between study blocks will perform better than learners who study without rest or diversion.

To make use of this knowledge, make each study block at least 40 minutes and no more than 60 minutes in length. Between these effective study blocks take a 5- to 10-minute break. When resting, do something active (i.e., walking, stretching) to get your mind off the material for a few minutes. Do not watch television or take part in any other distracting activity that may prevent you from ending your break.

If you feel you are "on a roll" with the material (i.e., really getting into the story of a book or comprehending the lesson of a textbook) do not feel pressured to take a break. Be realistic. If you find that you are losing focus or getting a bit tired, take a quick break. Yet, always strive to hit the 40-minute mark; otherwise your studying will only consist of breaks.

There are two main reasons students do not take breaks: (1) they feel breaks only slow the progress of their studying; and (2) they are afraid of not returning to their work after the break is done. Now that you know that effective learning occurs during distributed practice, it is evident that breaks actually increase the effectiveness of your study sessions. Additionally, breaks will help maintain your focus, composure, and endurance in the long run.

For those students who fear that they will evade studying by taking elongated breaks, you can remedy this issue by placing responsibility in somebody else's hands. Ask your roommate or a friend to remind you to get back to your work after your break. Or you can use a timer to regulate your study blocks and breaks. Let that timer be a reminder of the exact period you need to study. Don't rely on simply *looking* at a watch or clock because you can easily mentally shorten your study period ("I'll only study until 5:45 instead of 6:15") or extend the time of your break ("I think my break should last until the television show is over").

Really effective students set manageable goals for their study periods. Each time you study, try setting a realistic action goal that can be achieved in the time allotted. Setting unrealistic goals will only discourage you when they are not met. Setting reasonable action goals for each study session will motivate you to achieve.

PART II: DEVELOPING YOUR PERSONALIZED STRATEGIES

Deeper Learning

Learning occurs on a spectrum of levels. In your studies, aim for the third (formation of concepts, ideas, or principles) or fourth (understanding) level of learning. Develop active learning techniques that will allow you to achieve these higher stages of knowledge.

NOTES

1. Robert C. Pace, "Measuring Quality of Effort," Laboratory for Research on Higher Education (Los Angeles: UCLA, 1979).
2. Benson R. Snyder, *The Hidden Curriculum* (Cambridge: MIT Press, 1973).
3. Based on Edgar Dale, *Audio-Visual Methods in Teaching,* 3rd ed. (New York: Holt, Rinehart & Winston, 1969), 108. While Edgar's (and others') chart shows percentages corresponding to each learning activity, Genovese's article, "The Ten Percent Solution" (see bibliography), indicates that no actual research supports such percentages. Even Edgar describes the chart as "merely a visual aid to explain the interrelationship of the various types of audio-visual materials, as well as their positions in the learning process." The chart has been provided without the percentages because it still accurately displays increasingly active approaches to learning.
4. C.L. Hull, *Principles of Behavior* (Englewood Cliffs, NJ: Prentice Hall, 1943). Clark (see bibliography) summarizes Hull's findings as follows:

    Hull (1943) discovered that when *practice periods are spaced apart (distributed practice), performance is superior to what it is when practice periods are close together (massed practice). Also, during practice periods, the learners' performance will gradually improve until some asymptotic (maximal) level is reached. If the learners are allowed to rest, and then resume practice, their performance will tend to exceed their previous asymptotic level (reminiscence effect). Learners that are provided rest or some other form of diversion between practice periods will reach higher levels of performance than learners who practice straight through without rest or diversion.*

BIBLIOGRAPHY

Clark, Donald. *A Few Good Learning Theories.* May 29, 2000. http://www.nwlink. com/~donclark/hrd/learning/theories.html (January 15, 2005).

Dale, Edgar. *Audio-Visual Methods in Teaching.* 3rd ed. London: International Thomson Publishing, 1969.

Genovese, Jeremey E.C. "The Ten Percent Solution." *Skeptic* 10, no. 4 (2004): 55–57.

McKeachie, Wilbert J. "Research on College Teaching: The Historical Background." *Journal of Educational Psychology* 82, no. 2 (1990): 189–200.

McKeachie, Wilbert J. *Teaching Tips: Strategies, Research, and Theory for College and University Teachers.* Lexington: D.C. Heath, 1994.

Miller, Dean et al. "Effects of Learning Styles and Strategies on Academic Success." *Journal of College Student Personnel,* no. 28.5 (1987): 399–404.

Pace, C. Robert. "Measuring Quality of Effort." Laboratory for Research on Higher Education. Los Angeles: UCLA, 1979.

Schuell, Thomas J. "Cognitive Conceptions of Learning." *Review of Educational Research* 56, no. 4 (1986): 411–436.

Snyder, Benson R. *The Hidden Curriculum.* Cambridge: MIT Press, 1973.

Weinstein, Claire E., and Richard E. Mayer. "The Teaching of Learning Strategies." *In Handbook of Research on Teaching,* 315–327. New York: Macmillan, 1986.

Wittrock, Merlin C. "Students' Thought Processes." *In Handbook of Research on Teaching,* 297–314. New York: Macmillan, 1986.

NAME: ______________________________ DATE: ____________________

JOURNAL QUESTIONS

Discuss the importance of your quality of effort while studying.

Define and give examples of active learning.

Why should you probably not study in your room?

Where is a good place on or near campus to study?

How long is an effective study block? Why should you take breaks?

How can office hours motivate you to be a better listener?

NAME: ______________________________ DATE: ____________________

EXERCISE 1. PERSONALIZED METHODS

Write down personalized methods that seem plausible to you for the topics in the chart.

STRATEGIES TO . . .	MY PERSONALIZED TECHNIQUES
enhance critical thinking	• • • •
utilize all three modes of learning	• • • •
utilize my mind style learning preference	• • • •
achieve deeper levels of learning	• • • •
be a better reader	• • • •
be a better listener	• • •

Chapter 7

Survival Note Taking

Pencils, Books, and Teachers' Dirty Looks

Will this be on the final?

—SCENE FROM EVERY COURSE EVER TAKEN THROUGHOUT ACADEMIC HISTORY

NAME: ____________________ DATE: ____________

WRITING ACTIVITY 1

Think for a moment about the way that you take notes for classes. Write down your top *four* strategies for taking effective notes.

How did you do? Unfortunately, if you're like most students, you simply put "I write down whatever the professor says." This is a recipe for disaster. Without time for preparation and review, note taking can be an incredibly *inefficient* way of understanding course material. What we present below is a more efficient way to take course notes that will save you time, facilitate your understanding, and hopefully increase your retention of class material so that you will perform better on course exams.

Did we promise you enough? Let's go!

Flashback. How many times have you seen the following situation? A student walks into class late after the professor has already begun lecturing. She noisily places her backpack on the desk and then fumbles for pen and paper. After not finding them, she interrupts one of her classmates to borrow something. She finally settles in to listen to the lecture; however, she has difficulty understanding it since she has begun in the middle. As time goes by, her attention drifts off to everyday activities and problems. When she does realize that something important has been said, she tries to write it down verbatim, and when this proves to be impossible, she gets frustrated and gives up. At the end of class she leaves and never thinks about her notes again until the night before the exam. *Then, when she looks at her notes, they make absolutely no sense and do not help her with exam preparation.* She blames her professor for being unclear in the presentation of material.

Does this sound familiar?
Have you done any—or all—of these things?
What is wrong with this student's note taking method?

Taking notes is one of the most valuable skills in the academic enterprise. Williams and Eggert (2003) found that accurate note taking was highly predictive of positive exam performance. You would think that, given its importance, note taking skills would be well-rehearsed and frequently discussed. However, many students know very little about effective note taking and assume that it is something that will just happen naturally. *Wrong!* The good news is that note taking is a skill, and with a little thought and practice you can improve your abilities substantially. We will present the process of effective note taking in four easy steps: ***preparing to take notes, taking notes, reviewing your notes, and evaluating your notes.***

PREPARING TO TAKE NOTES

In the example given above, the student was wholly unprepared to take notes. How about you? Did you mention anything about *preparation* as one of your top four strategies above? We find that the lack of preparation is a common reason why students take poor notes. Just as you would prepare for having a party or going on a date, you also need to prepare for taking notes in a class. Here are some guidelines on how to become prepared to take notes.

Read the Material

Unfortunately, to many of our students the idea of "reading ahead" has almost become a joke. If you are doing great in your courses, you probably don't need to worry about it. However, if you are struggling like many do, reading ahead can be a big help. Read the material before the class in which it will be discussed. Usually, it is obvious what the topic of discussion will be for a class period. If you are unsure of the topic, ask the professor beforehand. Then, read the textbook material corresponding to that topic. Reading ahead costs you no extra time, since you have to read the material anyway. However, by reading it beforehand, you will have a context for taking class notes. This is infinitely more efficient. Material will not seem as new, and you will be able to ask intelligent questions and clarify uncertainties you have from the lecture or reading.

Take Down the Outline

Many professors provide an outline on the board or an overhead prior to the class lecture. *Be sure to write it down.* Then, as you are taking notes, you can fill in the outline, using the same level of hierarchy and structure as provided. This can be a tremendous help if the professor tends to wander during course lectures. (Yes, it does happen!) Also, if something is missing or unclear, you can ask the professor where it fits on the outline. Similar to reading the material beforehand, using an outline provides you with a context for taking better notes. A final advantage is that the outline alerts you when the professor proceeds from one topic to another, helping you to avoid a minute or two of confusion trying to figure out where the lecture is going.

Review Your Notes

While you're waiting for class to begin, use your time wisely and review your notes from previous lectures. Doing so not only gives you a context for the day's lecture (which facilitates improved note taking), it is also an excellent way to study. If you frequently review your notes prior to class, you will find that you already have learned much of the material when it comes time to prepare for an exam.

Take Charge of Your Environment

For the student example given above, the student obviously was not ready to take notes. She not only hurt herself, she disrupted the class for those around her. How about you? Do you set up an ideal environment in which to take notes? If you are unsure, here are some useful tips.

- Get to class early if possible, allowing you time for review and preparation.
- Have your pens and notebook ready.
- Sit in a place that helps you pay attention. For most of us, this is in *the front of the class.* Sitting in the back of the class with the other disruptive, unprepared students can be a major mistake.
- Preparing yourself physically and emotionally can also go a long way in helping you pay attention and take good notes.

NAME: ______________________ DATE: ______________

WRITING ACTIVITY 2

Honestly discuss how much time you put into the preparation for taking notes. Which techniques are you going to begin using now that you know about them? Are there other strategies you need to consider that are helpful for specific classes? Set some realistic goals for future classes.

TAKING NOTES

Now that you are finally ready, let's take some notes. We find ***two major mistakes*** occur at this stage of the process. First, some students ***take no notes at all!*** Each of us has had the experience of giving a detailed list on the chalkboard or an overhead and, upon turning around, finding that some students are taking no notes. It isn't that they are not listening (although there certainly are always a few of these people). They just choose not to take notes. If we see these students during office hours (often because they did poorly on an exam), we ask why they don't take notes. They state that note taking interferes with their listening. They believe that if they just listen, they will magically absorb the material and be able to provide it to us at exam time. This is a myth. Research indicates that incredibly few students are able to just absorb and remember the material without taking notes—many can't even recall details of the lecture immediately after class! We have yet to meet the student who can do so.

The other major mistake we see is the student who tries to ***write down everything verbatim.*** Of course, it's impossible. Inevitably, the student ends up leaving out what escapes the brain prior to being recorded rather than selectively recording the lecture's important points. And there's no time to ask either! The student may even record a lecture and then try to write down everything verbatim. This is an inefficient, time-consuming strategy destined to fail if you have even a few other demands in your life. Yes, we would like you to have a life! Therefore, we propose a *compromise avoiding both mistakes.* Take relevant, efficient notes that are of great benefit in exam preparation. To help you do so, here are a few ideas for taking effective notes.

Be Active Rather Than Recording Material Verbatim

When taking class notes, it is important to process the material actively and not just be a passive word writer. Think about what is the *most* important thing being said—an outline on the board or an overhead often helps you choose this point. Discriminate between important material that you will need to know later and your professor's ramblings that just fill in space. *This is a skill that improves over time, so don't be discouraged if you can't do it now.* Our senior teaching assistants have often remarked how inefficient first-year students are in understanding what is important. What these seniors often don't realize is how well they have developed this skill over their four years of college. It will get better with practice, but you do have to pay attention and work on it. (This is also why reading text material prior to class is so important for providing context for understanding the day's lecture!)

Ask Yourself Questions

As you are listening and preparing to write, ask yourself questions about the material. For example, what is the point the professor is trying to make? How likely is this to be on the exam? Does the professor value this area? Effective note taking, and later on effective test taking, is in some ways an interpersonal skill of getting to know your professor. You need to discover a professor's goals, patterns, intentions, and biases. You can process some of this information early on while taking notes. Later, you can assess how effective your guesses were by thoroughly reviewing your exam.

Ask Your Professor Questions

One exceedingly simple strategy for taking more effective notes is to ask questions when the material seems unclear. Simple, yet underused. How about you? Are you willing to ask questions in class if something isn't clear? How about just asking the professor to repeat something or to slow down? This also takes some interpersonal skill and some assertiveness. The old adage is usually true: if you don't understand something, it is likely that others don't understand it either. If you have difficulty speaking up in class, we suggest that you sit by a more assertive classmate. When you have a question, get him or her to ask it. Or be expressive, which only works if you sit where a professor sees you well. If you frown, look mixed up, or shake your head, some professors will repeat points or ask if you have a question. It's easier to ask a question if you have actually been asked to do so by a professor.

Figure Out the Main Points in Today's Lecture

In most lectures of less than an hour, there are a *maximum of four or five central points.* Attempt to identify what these main points are. Then, you can fit the rest of the data and examples as supporting material for these main points. Again, this process will keep you active in your note taking and help you identify the material that the professor values.

Use Abbreviations—and Be Sure You Can Remember What They Mean!

It is amazing to watch students taking notes in a beautiful, longhand script as though they were writing a note to a close admirer. The process of effective note taking is often a race against time. Establish a system of abbreviations and symbols to help you in this race. If you don't know a number of common abbreviations, it may be helpful to look in a shorthand textbook. You also might ask classmates and friends some of the abbreviations they find helpful. Some disciplines also have their own set of codes and symbols, and you would do well to learn them. Finally, it can be fun spending some time making up your own verbal shortcuts. Whatever system you choose, be sure to write clearly so that you will be able to understand it when you review. If you miss a class, asking to borrow notes from a student who takes good notes will introduce you to new abbreviations. This situation will give you a chance to practice asking questions and learn some new, useful shortcuts!

Pace Yourself

We mentioned earlier the benefits of using an outline from the board or an overhead. This is useful when pacing yourself during a lecture. When using a hierarchy, you can indent to identify points supporting the main topic. In addition, you can leave a space when you fall behind, but go back and fill it in when the professor pauses or begins some examples. Again, don't overlook the option of asking the professor to slow down. Be sure to fill in the holes in your notes at your earliest opportunity. Just be aware that professors seldom use an "English" outline, always having a "b" to go with an "a."

Take Down Examples—and Make Up Your Own

We often see students taking notes furiously while the professor is giving terms and definitions. However, once the instructor begins to give an example, students put their pens down and use it as an opportunity to take a brief nap. ***Don't do this!*** First of all, the example may be the very thing that helps you understand the term. In addition, on exams many instructors use application-type questions that require your understanding of the example or ask you to provide a new one. Therefore, we recommend that you write down enough of the example to understand it when you are reviewing your notes. Understanding a professor's example serves as a framework for constructing new examples.

NAME: ______________________________ DATE: ____________________

WRITING ACTIVITY 3

Answer all of these questions, and then rate your note taking ability on a scale from 1 to 100. How well are you able to keep up with the information presented in your classes? How coherent are your scratchings when it comes time to review for an exam? Which of the previous strategies do you employ? What are your strengths and weaknesses? Finally, set some realistic goals for improvement *prior to the next class.*

Consider the Special Case of Missing a Class

As you can see, the process of taking effective notes is something that is established over time. It is also something very unique to your style of taking notes and understanding of the professor. Therefore, getting notes from other students when you have missed a class can be disastrous. Most students are not good note takers. Even getting the professor's notes can be less than ideal as they are related to his or her unique understanding of the topic and sometimes only consist of a few words, each of which triggers several minutes of lecture material. If you miss class, you might ask the professor to recommend a good note taker from whom you can borrow the notes.

A related point is the importance of attending class. Many find the time spent attending class to be less than that spent reconstructing a friend's notes. Also, we believe that going to class is a highly efficient use of one's time. You get to hear what the professor emphasizes and learn which information is highly valued. Often, the examples can only be understood in the context of the class. We performed a study (Beck, Koons, & Milgrim, 2000) assessing which variables predicted success in a mass lecture General Psychology course. ***We found the variable that was the best by far at predicting course grades was class attendance.***

REVIEWING YOUR NOTES

For most students, class notes remain untouched from the time they are taken until the night before the exam. *Big mistake!* How about you? How often do you look at your notes prior to your last-minute panic? It is imperative that you spend some time reviewing your notes as soon as possible after taking them. Doing so provides another opportunity for learning, serves as a context for future notes, and highlights information that may need to be clarified. Below are some suggestions for reviewing your notes.

Review Your Notes as Soon as Possible after the Lecture

Take a page from business managers and counselors, who write down the main points of a meeting *right after its occurrence* to remind themselves what was said and what they need to do about it. So take a few minutes after class to review and add to your notes. Here's a scary fact—short-term memory lasts less than 20 seconds unless you ***rehearse*** (repeat) it, which helps explain why taking no notes is a fatal error!

Unfortunately, most students wait until the night before the exam to review their notes. Abbreviations, examples, and linkages that made sense during a lecture have long since been forgotten. Information fades from awareness quickly unless you *actively* rehearse it, consolidating it into long-term memory. ***Active rehearsal*** isn't verbatim repetition; it requires you to put notes into your own words, explain them to yourself, and make whole sentences. Therefore, as you will have to look at your notes anyway, save yourself some time and review your notes as soon as possible. Look for holes in your notes while the lecture is still relatively fresh in your mind.

Actively Process the Material While You Are Reviewing

We often tell students just to read the material as soon as possible, and there is quite a benefit to doing so. However, if you really want to be efficient with your time, actively process your notes while you are reviewing them. What we mean is that rather than just reading the notes and filling in missing information, look again for main themes and linkages. If necessary, reorganize your notes when you have new insights about what the professor was trying to communicate. Some students like to retype their notes. While we think that a passive retyping of information can be an inefficient use of time, we have seen some recent computer-based voice recognition systems that speed up this process substantially (provided that you speak clearly so you don't have to retype mistakes). Use whatever system that works in keeping you actively engaged with the material.

Clarify Unclear Information

One of the real benefits of reviewing your notes is to assess whether you understand what has been presented. This, however, is only part of your task. If you are uncertain about anything, it is *your responsibility* to clarify the information. Asking the professor for clarification has a number of benefits. First, it ensures that your notes are clear, providing a structure for studying. Second, it communicates interest to your professor, which may provide a foundation for future learning and recommendations. As we said before, if you didn't understand the material, it is likely that many of your classmates didn't either. Finally, you are spending a lot of money and effort pursuing a quality education. *Be assertive in ensuring that you get just that!*

EVALUATING YOUR NOTES

Even if you are on the right track, you'll get run over if you just sit there.

—ANONYMOUS

Finally, even with all these steps, you need to assess your level of note taking ability. The most obvious indicator of this is whether you are performing well on the portion of your exams that come from class lectures. If you are doing *really well,* your note taking technique is probably sufficient—at least for this class! If your grades are poor, you need to decide where you are going wrong and correct it *now.* Here are ideas for evaluating your notes.

Get Feedback from Others

Compare your notes with those of peers and/or teaching assistants. See whether you have the same coverage of important information. How clear is your content? How effective and memorable are your abbreviations and symbols? Is your organization sufficient? Do your self-originated examples really fit the material? You may also benefit from showing your notes to your course professor. Just be sure to do so well before an exam so that feedback will be useful.

Take a Course

Most universities have courses on study skills and note taking, in addition to other student support services. The time invested (which may even qualify for credit toward graduation) can pay off dramatically in future performance and time savings. Again, note taking is a skill that can always be improved. Get a jump on the competition by honing this skill!

Consider an Additional Resource: The Cornell Note Taking System

A well-known and more formalized system of note taking was developed by Walter Pauk (2000) over 40 years ago for students at Cornell University. It incorporates many of our suggestions in a more stylized format. Many students have used it successfully. There are hundreds of excellent references to the "Cornell Note Taking System" on the Internet that explain how you can use it. We also give a citation for his book in the references below.

LOOKING BACK AND GETTING A LIFE

We hope you have already begun to benefit from the suggestions in this chapter. We also hope that sensitizing you to the complete process of note taking will make you a better student with fewer academic stressors. The idea is to let you do effective and efficient school work that will provide you with *both academic satisfaction* ***and*** *more free time for friends, activities, and yourself.* We challenge you to give it a shot. Once you see the values of enhanced note taking, please provide us with feedback about what worked for you.

REFERENCES

Beck, B. L., Koons, S. R., & Milgrim, D. L. (2000). Correlates and consequences of behavioral procrastination: The effects of academic procrastination, self-consciousness, self-esteem and self-handicapping. *Journal of Social Behavior and Personality*, 15(5), 3–13.

Pauk, W. (2000). *How to study in college* (7th ed.). Boston: Houghton Mifflin.

Williams, R. L., & Eggert, A. (2003). Notetaking predictors of test performance. *Teaching of Psychology*, 29, 234–237.

SUGGESTED WEB SITES

http://ub-counseling.buffalo.edu/stressmanagement.shtml This site provides information on a variety of topics for college students (e.g., stress, study skills, procrastination, perfectionism, time management).

http://www.unc.edu/depts/unc_caps/resources.htm The University of North Carolina's Counseling And Psychological Services presents practical information on academic improvement, eating disorders, substance abuse, depression, sleep, grief, stress management, assertiveness, and helping a friend. You can access other sites from this page too.

http://www.thesemester.com Tips on how to successfully complete the semester are offered.

http://www.collegefreshman.net This site has insightful information about college life and even allows you to talk with other first-year students. It has tips on dealing with college coursework, roommates, and stress/health issues.

NAME: ______________________________ DATE: ____________________

WRITING ACTIVITY 4

What do you now realize are your top four note taking skills? Are they the same as those you listed at the beginning of the chapter?

Chapter 8

Credit Cards and Cash Management

PAPER OR PLASTIC?

How many times do we hear that question when bagging our groceries? It's not only a good question when sacking purchases, but it's also a good question to consider when paying for them.

Few things are as easy as whipping out a credit card and charging goods or services. Buying something we really want gives us pleasure and credit cards help fuel that feeling of instant gratification—until the bill arrives at the end of the month. Then, the pleasure is gone. Paying bills isn't fun and the goods we got some pleasure out of during the first of the month are limiting our spending power at the end of the month—and for many months to follow! Like a light switch, immediate gratification can turn on us quickly, temporarily or permanently disrupting our financial future.

Credit cards are generally used to bridge the gap between what we want and what we can afford to buy, especially when living on a limited budget. And, hey, it looks impressive to pull out a gold or platinum card to buy lunch at a restaurant. But, do you realize paying with credit is similar to taking out a bank loan to buy that burger or pizza? And, by placing no constraints on buying on credit, we can lead ourselves into financial trouble that is hard to escape.

It's hard to believe how accessible credit is these days. If gaining credit card offers were an Olympic sport, we'd all be on the medal stand. Most of us are bombarded daily with preapproved offers, transfer balance offers, checks that just need a signature to be activated, and the like.

Some people are even calling for Congress to pass legislation reducing the aggressive marketing tactics used by many credit card companies, especially the strategies used with high school and college students. Such legislation would not be necessary if we would learn how to "Just Say NO!" Just because they mail us an offer doesn't mean we have to accept. (And by the way, be careful about just tossing all those offers in the trash. Someone may use them to steal your identity and ruin your credit ratings! Be sure to shred all offers before tossing.)

Good credit is invaluable; bad credit is tragic. While credit can be a great financial tool, it can also be easily abused and take us so deep into debt that it takes years to recover. And overspending on credit cards is a certain financial death wish.

Using credit makes spending very impersonal. It allows us to buy and buy, without stopping to physically count the total amount of those expenditures. Only when we max out a credit card do we think about it being finite—and then most companies will simply increase our credit limit or just charge us for exceeding it. Basically, buying on credit is like having an endless supply of money to fund an endless flow of spending. Buying with cash is different. When the money is gone, the spending stops. Seeing the total amount of cash in our hands helps us better manage our spending habits because we know exactly what we have—and when it will be gone. Coins and currency are tangible; they are real—made from paper and metals. Credit cards are plastic and they represent pretend money; we pretend to have more money than we do.

Living with debt is not pleasant. It simple terms, we are using today's money to pay for yesterday's purchases. And, if that habit continues, we will always have trouble making ends meet. Financial goals become financial myths because it is virtually impossible to save when we are swimming in debt.

Any pleasure received from the purchase is offset by the increased stress of paying the bills. But it doesn't take much imagination to realize that stress from indebtedness takes away from our quality of life, often leaving us with strained relationships with family and friends, depression, or even thoughts of suicide.

If money rocks, then credit rolls. And for most of us, the balance on our credit cards rolls over from one month to another—compounding the interest and increasing the total amount we owe even when we're working to make the payments. The key is learning to manage debt, not having debt manage you.

CURRENT STATISTICS

In 1998, a study by the Education Resources Institute found that almost two-thirds of all college students have at least one credit card, while 20 percent of them have four or more credit cards (Education Resources Institute, June 1998).

DID YOU KNOW . . .

The average family has about $8,000 in credit card debt, and about $1,000 of their annual income goes to pay the interest on that debt every year. In fact, over 90 percent of the money a family spends goes toward paying past debt. Credit card debt in the United States grew at an annual rate of 9.2 percent between 1993 and 2003, compared with a 5.2 percent annual increase in personal income.

Source: Consumer Federation of America, 2000.

Students with high credit card debt face greater problems than just repaying the debt. Recent studies show that increased credit card debt requires students to work more hours to pay down their debt. Taking on the additional responsibility often leads to poor academic performance—and in some cases, it actually requires students to drop out of college or take a reduced load, postponing their graduation dates in order to repay their credit card debt.

But that's not all. Taking fewer hours and an extra year or two to graduate may also increase the cost of going to college!

Adding more problems, students with high credit card debt have a much harder time repaying student loans once they do graduate.

Furthermore, some employers and graduate schools will actually reject applications from students who had bad credit while in college. And, poor credit ratings make it difficult to lease an apartment, buy a car, or purchase a home once students enter the workforce.

So, before you charge that late-night pizza or download the latest hit, think about the potential long-term consequences of your choice!

In 2000, a study by Nellie Mae reported an increase in those numbers. Their survey found that 78 percent of undergraduates (aged 18–25) and 95 percent of graduate students had at least one card. Undergraduates carried an average balance of $2,748 while graduate students carried an average balance of $4,776. Nellie Mae also found that of the 78 percent of undergraduates with a card; 32% had four or more cards; 13% had credit card debt between $3,000 and $7,000; and 9 percent had credit card debt greater than $7,000 (Nellie Mae, 2000).

LIVIN' LARGE: MANAGING CREDIT

1. Pay your bills on time. Missing a payment will result in additional fees plus higher interest rates, which quickly compound and create more problems.
2. Credit cards are not all bad. They are convenient and safer to carry than cash, and they are a great tool for establishing a good history needed for future credit needs. Credit cards are not a substitute for income. Having good intentions to pay off credit cards is not the same as really paying them off! So, think twice before saying "CHARGE!"
3. Practice discipline when using credit, especially credit cards. They have a purpose and should be used only when absolutely necessary or if you have the money in the bank to pay them off each month. A good rule to use is this: Don't buy anything that takes longer to pay off than the product will last.
4. Read your statement and credit terms carefully. That small print is important! And, not all credit cards are the same.

5. Making minimum payments increases the cost of every purchase you make! Just because an item is on sale doesn't mean you have to buy it—especially if you are charging it to your credit card.
6. The only way to get out of debt is to stop spending. No one said it would be fun, but you must stop the bleeding before you can heal.
7. Carrying multiple credit cards is like playing Russian Roulette. There is incredible incentive to use them if they are in your pocket. Find a credit card with a moderate balance and the lowest possible interest rate. If you feel like you need an extra card "just in case," put it on ice. (Put extra cards in a container of water and put the container in your freezer. You can thaw them in case of emergencies. But the time delay gives you time to think—while still giving you the added security of another card.)
8. Keep your credit receipts and balance your card statement just like you balance a checking account. Yes, credit card companies do make mistakes. It also alerts you if someone else is using your card number without your knowledge.
9. If you have charges on multiple credit cards, pay off the one with the highest interest rate first. The easiest way to do this is by paying the minimum on all other credit cards, and paying as much as possible on the high-interest card. Once it is paid off, cut up the card and close your account. Then, add the amount you were paying to the second-highest-interest card and continue until all are paid off. Then, put that amount into your savings account so you won't need to rely on credit for future purchases.
10. If you know you are in credit trouble, get help. There are reliable credit counseling services available in most communities that can provide the assistance you need. If unsure where to go, talk to your banker or a financial advisor. It's probably wise to avoid unscrupulous firms who advertise on TV in the middle of the night.

NAME: ______________________ DATE: ______________

EXERCISE 1. CHOOSING A CREDIT CARD

Not all credit cards are the same. In fact, they vary greatly. Before taking out a credit card, think about how you will use it. Do you expect to pay your monthly bill in full? Carry over a balance from month to month? Use it for cash advances? Use it only for emergencies?

The answers to these questions will help you choose the best card for your needs.

Use the following checklist to compare three different cards. Information about most of these features is listed in the disclosure box that must appear in all printed credit card solicitations and applications.

Comparing Credit Cards

Features	*Card A*	*Card B*	*Card C*
What is the APR (annual percentage rate of interest) on each card for the following?			
Purchases?	______	______	______
Cash advances?	______	______	______
Balance transfers?	______	______	______
If you are late with a payment, does the APR increase?	______	______	______
If so, to what rate?	______	______	______
How long is the grace period			
If you carry over a balance?	______	______	______
If you pay off the balance each month?	______	______	______
For cash advances?	______	______	______
What are the fees?			
Annual?	______	______	______
Late payments?	______	______	______
Over the credit line?	______	______	______
Set up?	______	______	______
What are the cash advance features?			
Transaction fees?	______	______	______
Limits?	______	______	______

Features	*Card A*	*Card B*	*Card C*
How much is the credit limit?	______	______	______
What kind of card is it?	______	______	______
Secured, Regular, or Premium			
Does the card have other features?	______	______	______
Rebates	______	______	______
Frequent flyer miles	______	______	______
Insurance	______	______	______
Other	______	______	______

Based on a comparison chart available at http://www.federalreserve.gov/pubs/shop/checklist.htm

Chapter 9

Managing the Stresses of Life as a College Student

CASE STUDY

Nadir

Nadir and his wife have three boys between the ages of 6 and 12. Although he works full time, Nadir didn't think returning to college to get a degree would be too much for him. He signed up for two classes in the fall semester and plans to take three in the spring. However, it's near the end of the first semester, and he's already feeling the stress. He's highly motivated to succeed in college because he currently has a construction job and knows that he won't be able to do such a physically demanding job forever. His goal is to get into management or become a building inspector.

His job is somewhat seasonal, which gives him more time during the winter months to take classes, but the semester is not over when spring construction really picks up. Then the workload becomes intense. In addition, Nadir commutes to various job sites, which can add considerable time to his day. He would like to take more online or teleclasses, but most courses in his major are not offered in that format.

At home things are not all that stress-free either. Nadir's wife, Jennifer, and his recently widowed mother do not get along well. Some of their problems stem from cultural misunderstandings. He is an only son and feels a strong responsibility to take care of his mother. He knows that is what his father would have wanted him to do. His mother doesn't make it easy for him, though, as she expects Nadir to be at her beck-and-call every time she needs the least little thing done. She would never consider hiring strange workmen to come to her house. No; a good son should do whatever is needed.

All of the running around for his job and his mother doesn't leave Nadir much time for recreation, exercise, or to take care of the chores at his own house. He realizes he needs to spend quality time with Jennifer in order to keep their marriage strong. He would also like to spend more time with his boys. They need a father's influence and guidance, especially the preteen son.

The biggest stress of all is the approaching holiday season. Jennifer comes from a large family that has always made family gatherings the focal point of the holidays. A few years ago her parents divorced, and now her father is remarried. Celebrating with both of her parents adds to the already overcrowded schedule. At the same time, Nadir's mother expects them to spend the holidays with her, especially now that she is alone.

Nadir finds it difficult to concentrate on his studies and is struggling with his one-day-a-week algebra course. Not only is the class long, but the instructor covers several chapters at each session. Nadir is feeling quite anxious about the final exam. He needs to do well in order to build strong skills, pass the course with a "C" or better, and move on to the next math level.

Reflections

- What are some ways Nadir can spend time with his family while also taking care of his own needs?
- How might Nadir and Jennifer lessen the stress of the holiday season?
- What, if anything, can be done to help improve the relationship between Nadir's wife and mother?
- How can Nadir adjust his college schedule to accommodate all of the demands on his time?

INTRODUCTION

You probably didn't expect college to be easy, but many students are unprepared for how stressful going to college can be. As a college student, you are likely to have more roles than the average person. Most students work at least part time, but many are full-time employees. If you live at home, you probably have additional responsibilities. If you are married and/or a parent, you are aware of the time and energy involved in building strong relationships and running a household. If you're just starting to live on your own, you have the pressure of paying bills, grocery shopping, doing laundry, etc.—things that your parents used to do for you.

Many of you are also involved in activities either on campus or in the community. Now you've added the hours of homework and studying that it takes to maintain good grades. In addition, if you were not a strong student in high school, or if it has been a few years since you were in school, you might be feeling anxious about taking tests, working math problems, or writing papers. College courses move very quickly, and the pace frequently accelerates after midterm.

This chapter will help you *identify the things in your life that cause you stress.* In addition to college stressors, many people these days are trying to *deal with unreasonable feelings of anger.* Similar coping strategies are used in both anger and stress management. The *stress-reduction and relaxation techniques* introduced in this chapter may help you achieve balance in your life. *Math and test anxiety* are such common student stressors that a special section is devoted to ways of reducing them. So, if you're feeling a little stressed-out these days, read on; this chapter is for you.

Pretest

Identify the major changes that are happening in your life right now. Check as many as apply to you *within this past year.*

Family changes:

- Death of spouse, parent, sibling
- Death of grandparent or other close relative
- Divorce or marital separation (you or your parents)
- Marriage
- Pregnancy
- Gaining a new family member/s (birth, adoption, stepfamily, elder moving in, etc.)
- Major changes in health or behavior of a close family member

Health changes:

- Serious personal injury or illness
- Major change in sleeping habits
- Major change in eating habits
- Quitting, starting, or major increase in smoking, drinking, or other drug use
- Major change in amount of exercise or activities

Financial changes:

- Sudden loss of income
- Major change in financial status (a lot better or a lot worse-off than usual)
- Taking on a mortgage
- Foreclosure on a mortgage or loan
- Taking on a loan

Employment changes:

- Being fired
- Retiring
- Major change in work responsibilities (promotion, demotion, transfer)
- Changing careers
- Major change in working hours or conditions
- Major conflict with your boss/supervisor, or co-workers

Personal changes:

- Detention in jail or other institution
- Death of a close friend

- "Breaking-up" with girlfriend/boyfriend
- Conflict with spouse, in-laws, parents, or a close friend
- Beginning or ending formal education
- Moving to different residence/Major change in living conditions
- Outstanding personal achievement
- Revision of personal habits (dress, manners, associations, etc.)

Social changes:

- Changing to a new college
- Major change in usual type or amount of recreation
- Major change in church and/or social activities
- Vacation
- Major changes in holiday celebrations and/or number of family get-togethers

What does it mean? Change frequently causes stress. The more check marks—the more changes you have going on in your life—the higher your risk for a stress-related illness. If you have major changes taking place in all areas of your life (check marks in each category), that can also signal the potential for trouble.

WHAT IS STRESS?

Stress is the body's reaction to an occurrence or an event. You're driving to class and suddenly notice flashing lights and hear the siren of a police car behind you. Your body instinctively reacts. You look down at your speedometer; it shows 10 miles over the speed limit. Tension mounts. You prepare for what may follow. You don't really have time to stop and certainly can't afford a ticket. Your heart starts beating faster, and your mind is racing as you try to think of what to say. Even if the police car continues down the road, you may still feel a little shaken. Your adrenaline is high; you're stressed. A police car driving with its lights and siren turned on is not in itself a stressful event. If you were stopped at a red light on a side street or driving in the opposite direction, you would have a much different reaction to that event. The event is neutral, but your reaction to it can be positive or negative.

How we react in any situation is largely determined by our past experiences and our expectations of certain consequences or results. Our perceptions, beliefs, habits, level of self-confidence, and physical, mental, and emotional health also influence our reactions. No two people react exactly alike. What may be a challenge for one person may be distressful for another.

We usually think of stress as always being from negative or bad events, but stress also may occur from happy occasions. Starting college, planning a wedding, the birth of a child, celebrating the holidays with family, getting a new job, moving to a new house, or remodeling your current one are usually considered positive events. Yet, all of these can produce stress. *Change of any kind may produce stress.* That's why the pretest asked you to identify how many major changes are going on in your life right now. A little stress may be just what you need to motivate you. However, if you get too much stress in a very short time period, your body may become overloaded. When that happens, your natural immune system may be unable to defend itself against all of the germs, bacteria, and viruses that surround us. Your resistance is lowered, and you succumb to whatever illness is "going around." Being overloaded for a long period of time can be very damaging to your health. That's why it is important for you to use common sense and practice good health habits as your first line of defense.

Stress is unavoidable and affects everyone. Relationships with our families, friends, and others, as well as money, health, work, and college issues may all produce stress. Anger is a normal emotion that, if left unchecked, can result in serious problems. Major life events, everyday irritations, conflicts, and frustrations frequently result in feelings of anger that also boost our heart rate, adrenaline, and blood pressure levels. A specific event, such as a traffic delay that causes you to be late for class or work, or a specific person, e.g., a co-worker who is frequently late thus causing you to work overtime, both result in angry feelings that you need to resolve to eliminate further stress.

Sometimes we "set ourselves up" by developing unrealistic goals or setting our standards too high. When we expect too much of ourselves by overrating our abilities, we may fail to make satisfactory progress toward or not achieve our goals. Failure can produce a state of depression that prevents us from functioning effectively. The opposite is also true. We may set our standards too low or not try to achieve. Then, we're stressed by the consequences of our laziness and irresponsibility.

Another cause of stress is a conflict in our values. When we are in situations where we act contrary to our core beliefs and values, we feel the pressure of being phony. Time constraints or the feeling of always being overloaded is yet another huge stressor. When we lack the proper support and/or resources or feel that college or job demands interfere with our personal activities, we may exhaust our abilities to reduce or resist stress.

HOW TO REDUCE STRESS AND MANAGE YOUR ANGER

We cannot control all of life's stressors, but we can control our reactions to the people and events that cause us to become angry or stressed. Identify what is causing your stress, and then implement your own personal stress-reduction program. If you alter your beliefs and your way of thinking, you can reduce anxiety levels and their negative effects on your body. Stress is manageable, providing it does not approach a life-threatening level.

Step One: Look for Stress Symptoms—Be aware of the symptoms of anger and stress. Awareness always precedes action. Recognize the symptoms and don't deny that you have them. Be especially aware of times when you may "lose control" by using loud/abusive language, criticizing others, withdrawing socially, or inappropriately confronting others. You can start to solve the problem once you know it exists.

Step Two: Identify Stressful Times, Situations, and People—Identify the times and places when stress strikes you. Did you respond strongly to any of the pretest items? Think of the current causes of stress or anger "triggers" in your life right now. If it helps, keep a diary to pinpoint problem issues. Record what happened and your reaction. Think of other possible ways you could have reacted. List the kinds of things that were helpful in relieving the stress or reducing your anger level.

Step Three: Eliminate Unnecessary Stress—Whenever possible, eliminate the causes of unnecessary stress. From your diary you might have noticed a pattern of things or people that always stress you. When you come to that situation/person again, try to change your response. Don't jump to conclusions, and refuse to let anger and frustrations take over. Then, avoid those stressful situations. "That's easier said than done," you say, but remember that you control your own actions and reactions.

Changing your physical environment or your timing may also help you reduce your stress.

- Plan a different route if traffic jams cause you to become tense or you tend to develop "road rage."
- Shop at "off-peak" hours if you hate waiting in line at the grocery or mall.
- Try to schedule discussions on important issues with family members, friends, or coworkers when you feel alert and refreshed rather than just reacting without thought.
- If possible, take ten minutes for "personal down-time" to be alone when you arrive home from work, and let the stress of the day fade away.
- Be sure to take a few minutes for yourself during your workday.

You cannot change someone else, but you can change yourself and your attitudes. Don't let conflict with your significant others become your way of life. It's too exhausting and frustrating. Learn new skills such as assertive communication to improve and soften all your relationships.

Step Four: Reduce the Effects of Unavoidable Stress—For the stress in your life that you can't eliminate, try to control and reduce its effects. Remember to keep your perspective. Think about how important this event really is. Will you even remember it next week? Next month? If not, why get upset about it? Keep your stress at a minimum, and don't overreact.

It may not be possible to reduce all of life's irritations. Keep in mind that reacting with anger is ultimately a choice. Angry responses such as yelling, hitting, or confronting others can be outright aggressive. They may also be passive-aggressive—for example, backstabbing, gossiping, or manipulating others.

People have successfully dealt with the stress in their lives by using some of the techniques listed in Table 1.

Relaxation and Anger Management Techniques

It is difficult to eliminate all the stress in your life, but you can learn to reduce your anger and control your frustrations or anxiety by practicing relaxation exercises. Some are more involved, but others are simple enough to do anywhere—even in the classroom. Try one or more of the following exercises whenever you feel yourself becoming angry, tense, or overly tired, or if you feel that others may be taking advantage of you.

Deep Breathing

Anger and stress result in shallow, rapid breathing. Deep, slow breathing can reduce stress and help you relax. Oxygen is the body's natural stress-reducer, and increasing your body's

Table 1 COMMON STRESS REDUCERS

ESTABLISH SUPPORT SYSTEMS	MANAGE YOUR TIME
• Keep the positive, supportive relationships you have and build new ones. • Ask for help when you need it. • Use available campus and community resources.	• Develop a schedule using "Time Management" techniques. • Simplify your life. • Learn to say "No" to requests that are not priorities. • Delegate when necessary. • Use mini "downtime" breaks.
PRACTICE EMOTIONAL CONTROL	**MAINTAIN A HEALTHY LIFESTYLE**
• Use assertive communication techniques to prevent anger/frustration from causing undue stress. • Eliminate self-defeating behaviors and keep things in perspective. • Practice forgiveness. • Use cooperation rather than confrontation to reach your goals. • Be willing to compromise and seek alternative solutions to problems. • Use humor and laughter to lighten your emotional load. • Seek professional counseling if necessary.	• Eat nutritionally-balanced meals. • Get plenty of sleep. • Exercise regularly. • Avoid using drugs, including alcohol and tobacco. • If sexually active, protect yourself and your partner from sexually transmitted diseases or from unwanted pregnancy. • Take time for yourself—do whatever you enjoy to help promote balance in your life. • Try massage therapy or other relaxation techniques.
UNDERSTAND YOURSELF	**ACCEPT CHANGE AND LEARN NEW SKILLS**
• Think through what you really believe and why you believe it. • Be open to new experiences and ideas. • Practice critical thinking when faced with decisions. • Use your faith for motivation and to guide you through difficult situations.	• Learn something new to energize and revitalize your spirit and to increase your productivity. • Accept change with a positive attitude and as an opportunity to grow.

oxygen intake helps relieve tension. Begin by closing your eyes. Exhale slowly, and clear the air from your lungs. Then inhale deeply through your nose and hold your breath for a count of five. When taking a deep breath, your stomach (actually, your diaphragm) should be expanded. Slowly exhale, using your lips to control the rate of air that you move out of your lungs. Begin the cycle again. Repeat several times until you feel calmer. You can do this anywhere and any time you feel stressed, whether you are taking an exam or confronting a family member or co-worker.

Deep Muscle Relaxation

One of the most common reactions to anger and stress is muscle tension. Think of a time when you've been very angry or frustrated, and remember the tenseness in your jaw, neck, shoulders, arms, and hands. Deep and progressive muscle relaxation will help you relax your entire body from head to toe by first tensing and then relaxing the various muscle groups. The whole process can take anywhere from one to twenty minutes.

Find a comfortable position either sitting or lying down. If you are alone, you may want to loosen any tight clothing. Close your eyes. Begin with your head and facial muscles—scalp, brow, eyes, lips, jaw, etc. Tighten your muscles and hold tense for ten seconds, then relax. Continue contracting and relaxing your muscles by moving through your neck, shoulder, back, and chest areas. Keep doing this through every major muscle group. Concentrate on your breathing (slow, deep breaths) while you work your way down to your hips, legs, and feet.

When you have completed all the muscle groups, you will feel refreshed, calm, and relaxed. This type of relaxation may also help you sleep better. You can do a shortened version of this exercise in class or almost anywhere. Close your eyes; tense up all of your muscles for a couple of seconds; then release them slowly, one body part at a time.

Meditation

An ancient relaxation technique—meditation—can help you clear stressful thoughts from your mind, but it may take time to learn how to do it effectively. Find a location where you are comfortable and won't be disturbed. Close your eyes and focus on a peaceful word or image. Your goal is to find a quiet, peaceful state of mind. Concentrate on something calming, and do not let any other thoughts enter your mind. Learning to abandon all other thoughts is the hard part. Return to the one image or word you have selected, clearing your mind of any stress and worry. Breathe deeply. At the end of your meditation session, you will feel calm and relaxed.

Imagery

Imagery is another type of mental exercise. It is like taking a mini, mental vacation or daydreaming with a purpose. You can achieve the same feeling of tranquility that you do with meditation, but the technique is different. Rather than concentrating on a single thought, you create an entirely relaxing, though imaginary, place of your own to which you can escape. Once again, close your eyes and visualize the perfect place to relax. It might be in the woods by a brook, on a warm, sandy beach, in the mountains, floating on a cloud—wherever seems right to you. See yourself there, calm and satisfied with life. You can go to this special place in your mind whenever you need a few seconds of escape-time. You can also use this technique to build confidence. While in your perfect place, visualize yourself accomplishing one of your goals.

Pampering Yourself

There are a variety of products currently on the market to help you relax. Everything from bubble bath to scented candles can be used to create a soothing environment. Relaxing music, pleasant aromas, multimedia that captures the sights and sounds of ocean waves, raindrops, a crackling fire, or any number of other auditory and visual images can produce a tranquil state of mind. Massage therapy is now readily available in a variety of forms—chair massages for the neck and shoulders, pulse or wave massages, and full-body massages.

STUDENT STRESSORS

Adjusting to new and unfamiliar situations is a cause of stress for most people, and students are no exception. A new college, new course, or new instructor may create a great deal of anxiety. How much depends on his/her personality and past experiences. For a student, quizzes, tests, and final examinations can induce stress. A more extreme form is called test anxiety. Another high stressor for students is their fear of math. Both of these kinds of anxiety could be caused by a history of not doing well in school or on tests, having poor study skills, fear of failure, and outside pressures.

Test Anxiety

It is not abnormal to be anxious about a test. Almost everyone feels some apprehension, fear, uneasiness, or worry about taking a test. A little pressure can be beneficial if it is moderate and controlled, and some students view an exam as an opportunity to show what they can do. Their attitude is similar to that of an athlete who enjoys competition because it enhances his/her own performance. If moderate anxiety keeps you alert and provides you with a burst of energy, it can help you do your best.

Test anxiety may result in noticeable physical symptoms such as headaches, nausea, sweating, or dizziness. It can reduce your ability to concentrate and make you feel overwhelmed and unable to perform. The anxiety is self-induced, but outside pressures to maintain good grades may be contributing factors. If you suffer from anxiety because you think you have to be perfect, you need to let go of some of your unrealistic expectations. When stress and anxiety become so extreme that they affect your performance or become detrimental and threatening to your well-being, however, you may need the help of a professional to get your anxiety under control. If your anxiety is less extreme, you may be able to use the following strategies to handle it yourself.

Test Anxiety Reduction

- **Attitude Adjustment**—Be realistic about the importance of any single test or exam. What is the worst that could happen? You could get a lower grade than you wished;

you could be embarrassed about your performance; you could fail the test; or a poor test grade could cause you to fail a course in which you are struggling. You might even lose an opportunity for a scholarship or have to pay back some of your financial aid. Yes; these are all terrible consequences, but none of them will determine the outcome of the rest of your life. A test is just a test—usually part of your total grade for one course in any one semester. Recognize that your value as a person is not dependent on what you do on any one test or in any one course.

- **Effective Study Techniques**—Previous chapters have introduced you to strategies and techniques designed to increase your ability to perform successfully in the classroom. Faithfully practicing the note-taking, time management, and test-taking strategies outlined in this book will give you the confidence you need to go into the test with a winning attitude. Be sure to use tutoring and other academic support services as needed.
- **Positive Self-Talk**—Negative thinking increases your anxiety levels. Recognize any self-defeating thoughts you might have and replace them with positive thoughts designed to increase your confidence levels. Believe that you have the ability to control what happens and visualize yourself doing your absolute best. Practice using positive statements to boost your confidence and self-esteem. In your mind, tell yourself, "I am well prepared; I am confident; I will do my best."

Math Anxiety

The physical and psychological reactions to math that affects performance in class and keeps you from remembering what you learned when taking a math test is termed math anxiety. It is usually the result of negative past experiences. Most students with math anxiety can trace its roots to a school experience that convinced them they could not be successful in mathematics. Sometimes the pressure to do well, or conversely, the excuse to do poorly, came from parents and/or other family members.

If you suffer from math anxiety, think about your first negative experience with math. Was it failing to learn the multiplication tables right away? Was it being made to stand at the board in front of the class until you could work out a difficult problem? Was it the result of someone telling you, "You'll never be good in math"? To combat the causes of math anxiety, you need to recognize their sources, reject the untrue things you've been programmed to believe, and adopt a new approach—a willingness to go at it with a fresh start. If math anxiety can be learned (and it is), then it can be unlearned.

Math Anxiety Reduction

Effectively reducing math anxiety requires most students to combat negative self-images about their ability to be successful in math by taking positive steps to change their attitudes. First, they must develop and practice strong math study skills. Each small success in math performance will build confidence levels.

How can you change a negative attitude about math? Start by examining the math myths listed in Table 2, and become aware that these common assumptions are, indeed, myths.

Table 2 FALSE ASSUMPTIONS ABOUT MATH

- Math is linear and logical; therefore, creative people cannot be good in math.
- There is only one right way to solve a math problem.
- Women are not good in math. It's genetic. Variation: No one in my family is good in math; therefore, I can't/won't be good in math.
- Math has no value in the real world.
- I haven't been good at math in the past, and it's too late for me to learn math now.
- Math is hard and boring.
- It doesn't help to ask questions because I won't understand the explanation anyway.
- I've always been good in English, so I can't expect to be good in math.
- Math isn't logical.

Now that you've recognized these math myths, take a look at the following **math facts**:

- Math is sequential, building upon itself, so it is important to study every day. Studying once a week will not produce the same results as keeping up daily, especially if you have a class that meets three or more times per week.
- The key to solving math problems is practice. Keep up with your homework and work the problems whether or not the instructor collects or grades homework.
- It is more important to understand the concepts, principles, and relationships than it is to memorize the formulas and work the problems.
- Choosing math courses that meet as many times a week as possible is to your advantage. Classes that meet only once or twice a week tend to produce stress, especially for students who do not excel at math. If you don't understand the material, you may have to wait a whole week to ask your questions. In a five-day-per-week course, fewer concepts can be presented per day, which gives you time to practice before moving to the next topic.
- Avoid taking math during accelerated summer sessions because these sessions are even more intense and move *much more rapidly* than the traditional fall/spring semester courses.
- Missing a math class can cause a real gap in your knowledge and understanding. Remember, math is sequential. Missing any material can cause confusion and lack of understanding.
- Math anxiety is learned, and it can be unlearned.

We've reviewed some common myths and some truths about math. If you have difficulties with math and/or math anxiety, how can you counteract any negative attitudes you may have developed? First, you need to examine your past math experiences. Can you remember the first time you felt unhappy with your math performance? If you can uncover the source of your negative attitude, you can work on changing it to a positive one. If your problems with math stem from knowledge gaps or not understanding some fundamental concepts, then you can correct them by working in a computerized learning center or taking a basic math course to learn what you don't know.

Take a look at your current attitude. Do you truly believe that you will never be successful at math, or are you willing to change your attitude? The following tips for improving math performance will help you build a stronger, more positive attitude.

- Confront any math myths you've held in the past and recognize that they are myths.
- Use the relaxation techniques and positive self-talk approaches discussed earlier in the chapter to help you develop a positive attitude about your math ability.
- Attend every math class, take good notes, and record all steps in the examples covered in class so you will remember them later.
- Ask questions in class and seek tutorial assistance as soon as you do not understand any material. *Don't get behind!* Remember that sequential process.
- Review as soon as possible after class.
- Before registering for your next math class, talk to other students and try to identify instructors who are receptive to questions, use cooperative learning techniques, review material prior to tests, and teach in a style that matches your learning style.

Do all of your assignments and the sample problems provided. Practice makes perfect.

Practice the following steps to help you solve math problems:

- Make sure you understand basic definitions, symbols, and other math terminology.
- Know and understand the formula being used.
- Read the problem aloud.
- Draw a picture to help you see relationships within the problem.
- Examine the problem. Ask,
  - What information is given?
  - Specifically, what do I need to find?
  - What do I need to do?
- Estimate the end result.
- Ask yourself if your answer makes common sense.
- Check your answer.
- Practice until you understand how to do that kind of problem perfectly and completely.

SUMMARY

We all live complicated lives and are faced with stress on a daily basis. Moderate amounts of stress are normal and sometimes can motivate us to do our best. Too much stress, however, can cause serious physical, emotional, and behavioral problems.

Math and test anxieties are common problems experienced by many students. Both are learned responses that can be unlearned. Practicing good study habits, having a realistic attitude about the importance of tests in our lives, practicing positive self-talk, using relaxation techniques, and dispelling the math myths we have been taught will help us create success experiences.

We need to acquire the skills necessary to control or eliminate excessive stress in our lives. A number of strategies to help you develop your own stress management program were covered in this chapter. Maintaining a healthy lifestyle, using support systems, and practicing relaxation techniques are especially effective. If you have very high stress levels that have lasted for long periods of time, seek professional help. Remember that you can reduce many of your life stressors by identifying the people and events that cause you stress. Change the things in your life over which you have control, and release the rest. Don't worry; be happy!

NAME: ______________________________ **DATE:** ____________________

JOURNAL QUESTIONS

In the case study, Nadir faced many stressors. Which of the suggestions in this chapter would help him deal more effectively with them?

Now think about your own life and continue your essay by writing a response to one or both of the topics below.

1. Do you have test or math anxiety (or both)? To what do you attribute your fear of taking tests and/or your problems with math? What do you need to do to overcome these fears? List several strategies you will use.
2. Identify the major causes of stress in your life. Describe how you can eliminate some of them and what strategies you will use to reduce the effects of stress that can't be eliminated.

NAME: ______________________________ DATE: ____________________

EXERCISE 1. ACADEMIC ANXIETY

When taking math or other difficult courses, how much effort do you make to ensure that you can be successful?

Check your responses to the following:

	Usually do	Sometimes do	Never thought about it
Course Selection			
I schedule my difficult classes at a time when I am most alert.	✓		
I choose instructors that match my learning style.		✓	
I schedule the next course in a sequence as soon as I complete the prerequisite course.	✓		
Preparing for and Taking Tests			
I keep up-to-date so I don't have to cram the night before the test.	✓		
I look over the entire test before I begin.	✓		
If necessary, I take the full amount of time allotted.	✓		
I carefully review and check my answers before I turn in the test.	✓		
When my tests are returned, I keep track of the kinds of mistakes I've made.		✓	
If I don't understand what I did wrong, I meet with the instructor after class or during her/his office hours to make certain I will be able to work a similar problem correctly (e.g., on the final exam).			✓
General Anxiety Issues			
I believe that I can be academically successful.	✓		
I recognize that preparedness will help lessen any anxiety.	✓		
I know and am willing to practice simple relaxation techniques.		✓	

Look at your responses in the "sometimes do" or "never thought about it" column. Outline the steps you can take so your responses will be "usually do" for your next test or when you next register for classes.

Being better prepared is a good contingency plan for the usually do.

NAME: Daniel Deering DATE:

CHAPTER 10 READING GUIDE: MOTIVATE YOUR WAY TO SUCCESS

FOCUS QUESTION: What is your current feeling toward being in college? Do you have more positive than negative feelings? Explain why you have the current feelings that you do.

I feel good, because I am taking steps to shape my future.

1. Complete Exercise 1 titled: Why Are You Here? After listing your five top reasons for being in school, explain why you chose them.

   Expand knowledge, get better pay, Will to succeed, desire to succeed, Better study skills. For a Better future.

2. Complete the worksheet on clarifying your values. Complete the paragraph that asks you to describe what goals you are setting for yourself that reflect your top value decisions.

3. Complete the Coat of Arms Exercise. What are the priorities in your life?

   Stable future, to contribute positively to my environment. I want happiness in all forms

4. How can it help you be successful when you recognize what is important to you?

   It gives you a to do list of your goal's making it achievable.

5. Read the seven characteristics of a successful college student. What two characteristics do you already possess? What two do you need to strengthen?

Goals be flexible, Goals be realistic /

6. Read about Maslow's Hierarchy of Needs. Do you agree that people need to satisfy their lower needs first in order to achieve the higher ones? Relate this to your own life. Which needs are currently being met in your life?

7. What is the difference between external and internal motivation?

8. Read about Todd. Do you believe that the external or the internal motivation that he received from the test score was the best motivator? Explain your answer.

9. What are the three types of goals?

Goals should be realistic	Example of a realistic goal
Goals should be measurable	Example of a measureable goal
Goals should be flexible	Example of a flexible goal
Goals should be specific	Example of a specific goal

10. Read the Critical Thinking paragraph. How can your long-term goal affect your short-term goal? Apply this to your own life using an example of your own long- and short-term goals.

____

____

____

____

11. Do you know anyone who is always negative? What are they like?

yes, it is horribly ~~&~~ depressing

Do you know anyone who is always positive? What are they like?

Bubbly, sweet, enegetic and a bit jaded

Which one would you rather be around?

The positive

Rate your attitude:

ALWAYS POSITIVE 1 2 3 (4) 5 6 7 8 9 10 ALWAYS NEGATIVE

12. What is the difference between being negative and being realistic about a situation?

both are skewed because they are both unrealistic and are ~~a~~ altered by personallity

Write a short summary paragraph of this chapter. Include three major points that you found important.

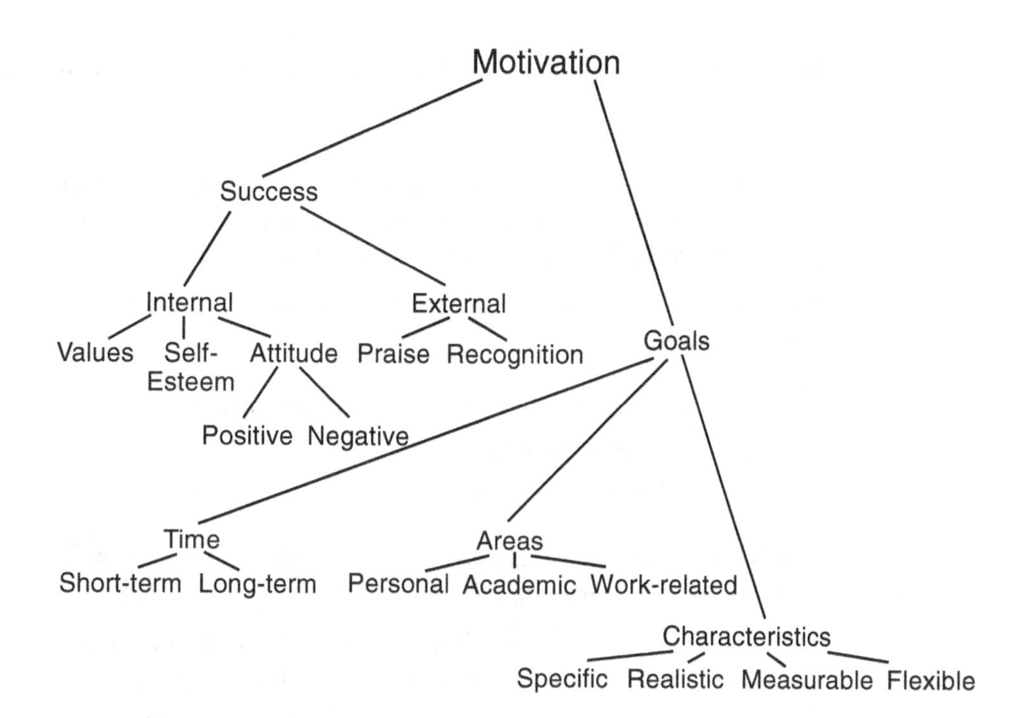

Chapter 10

Motivate Your Way to Success

WELCOME TO COLLEGE!

You have a lot of neat experiences ahead of you, some frustrating, and hopefully many rewarding. Are you excited about this new learning venture? Think back to your first day of elementary school. Do you remember how excited you were? Do you have that same enthusiasm today?

Unfortunately, many students associate learning with "school" and they don't have a lot of positive feelings toward school. Learning performance tends to drop as we go along in our academic pursuits. School is associated with "drudgery," and before we know it our attitude starts to be indifferent.

Let's try and start fresh with a good attitude like we had in first grade!

WHY ARE YOU HERE?

This is an important question for you to answer. There are several reasons why students attend college. Fill out Exercise 1 titled: Why Are You Here?

You need to stop and think about why you are in college. Are your reasons for being here due to others? Will these people be responsible for your success in life? Will they be attending class for you? Taking your tests? Receiving your diploma?

A recent study at a midwestern university revealed the top three reasons chosen for attending college were:

1. To increase the chances for a higher paying career
2. To expand knowledge
3. To help ensure success in life

This is a good time to examine your values and decide what you feel is important. Fill out the worksheet on clarifying your values. These values affect the choices you make in life.

The Coat of Arms Exercise will help you think about your personal feelings. Fill in this worksheet and think about the priorities in your life.

The student who is "educated" is the one who has learned how to learn. It is important to be aware of your values and goals because that will help motivate you to do your best. You need to recognize what is important to you, and strive to reach your potential. A college education can help you develop a flexible and open mind, sharpen your ability, and enrich your life.

WHAT IS A SUCCESSFUL COLLEGE STUDENT?

We all want to be successful. There is not one college student that attends college to be unsuccessful. How can we be successful? There have been numerous studies done in this area. Most of these studies show that successful students tend to possess the following characteristics:

1. *They have a definite reason for attending college.*

   You must decide what you want out of college. After completing the Exercise, Why Are You Here, you have had the opportunity to think about what is important to you.

2. *They have selected a vocation and are pursuing this course.*

   Don't panic if you don't have a career chosen. But, be aware that it provides motivation to have a career goal. Spend this first year trying out several courses in varying fields. Maybe one will ring a bell! When you have chosen your career, you will be motivated by a clearer sense of direction.

3. *They realize the need for understanding the material in each class and envision the value of it.*

   A successful student does not study just to pass a test. They usually have a three-pronged approach to the material.

   a. They master the basic facts. Without doing this, there is nothing on which to build.
   b. They take these basic facts and draw supporting details in for a total picture.

c. They learn to "think" with the subject. Once you are able to explain a concept in your own words—it's yours!

This approach allows them to "learn" the subject matter, not just memorize it.

4. *They have a desire for success.*

   The more success you experience, the more you will want.

   "Success Breeds Success"

   "Success Creates Interest"

   What a wonderful feeling accomplishment can bring! Have you ever failed a class that you really liked? Probably not. Success can create interest, which further ensures success. One way we have of achieving success is the attainment of goals. Much more about that later!

5. *They have the will to succeed.*

   Abraham Lincoln loved to read. It was told that he walked 20 miles to borrow a book. Would you exert that much effort? If we can't park close to the library, we probably will not bother to check out a book!

   How can we develop this kind of will to succeed?

   GOALS → SUCCESS → STRENGTHENS WILL → MORE SUCCESS

   We can develop this will to succeed by the attainment of short-term goals. Small successes strengthen our will, and the strengthened will provides us with additional power to work even harder.

6. *They have developed good study skills.*

   The definition of study skills is the efficient use of our mind and our time. The key word is "efficient." There are other phases of our life that need attention, and we need to develop study skills so we can accomplish the maximum in the minimum amount of time. Study skills are not instinctive, but something that we need to learn. The goal of study skills is independent learning. As long as you look to someone else for interpretation, you are not a free person intellectually.

7. *They know they must set priorities. "This is the time to learn."*

   Rank your needs at this time. It is not necessary for school to be number one, but it must be extremely high on the list.

   Consider this scenario:

   Greg was studying for a physics test. Doug and Jeff were on their way for pizza and a movie. They stopped by Greg's room and invited him along. Greg's decision could be crucial toward a high grade on his test the next day. What would you do?

WHAT IS MOTIVATION?

Webster's Dictionary defines motivation as the condition of being motivated; an incentive or drive. How do we apply this to ourselves? Let's think for a moment about ourselves.

How many brain cells do you have?

Hint: A lot more than you think!

You have 13 billion brain cells. Do you feel smarter already? One thing you should be thinking about right now is how to use these 13 billion cells to their fullest potential. In this book you will be able to find several effective ways to learn; ways that are the best for *you*.

Let's imagine that we have an assembled computer sitting in front of us. This computer contains one million parts.

What is the first thing we would need to do in order to use it?

Hint: Think electricity.

O.K., we should plug it in to the electrical outlet. What do we need to make our 13 billion part computer work? Our electric current is called *motivation*. Motivation is what makes learning come alive!

What Is Your Source of Motivation?

Our source of motivation is human needs. The psychologist Abraham Maslow believed that all human beings have a need to grow, to develop abilities, to be recognized, and to achieve. He viewed human needs in hierarchical order. Some needs take precedence over others. We need to satisfy the lower needs in order to achieve the higher ones (see Figure 1). If we don't take care of our fundamental needs which are our basic physiological needs (hunger, thirst,

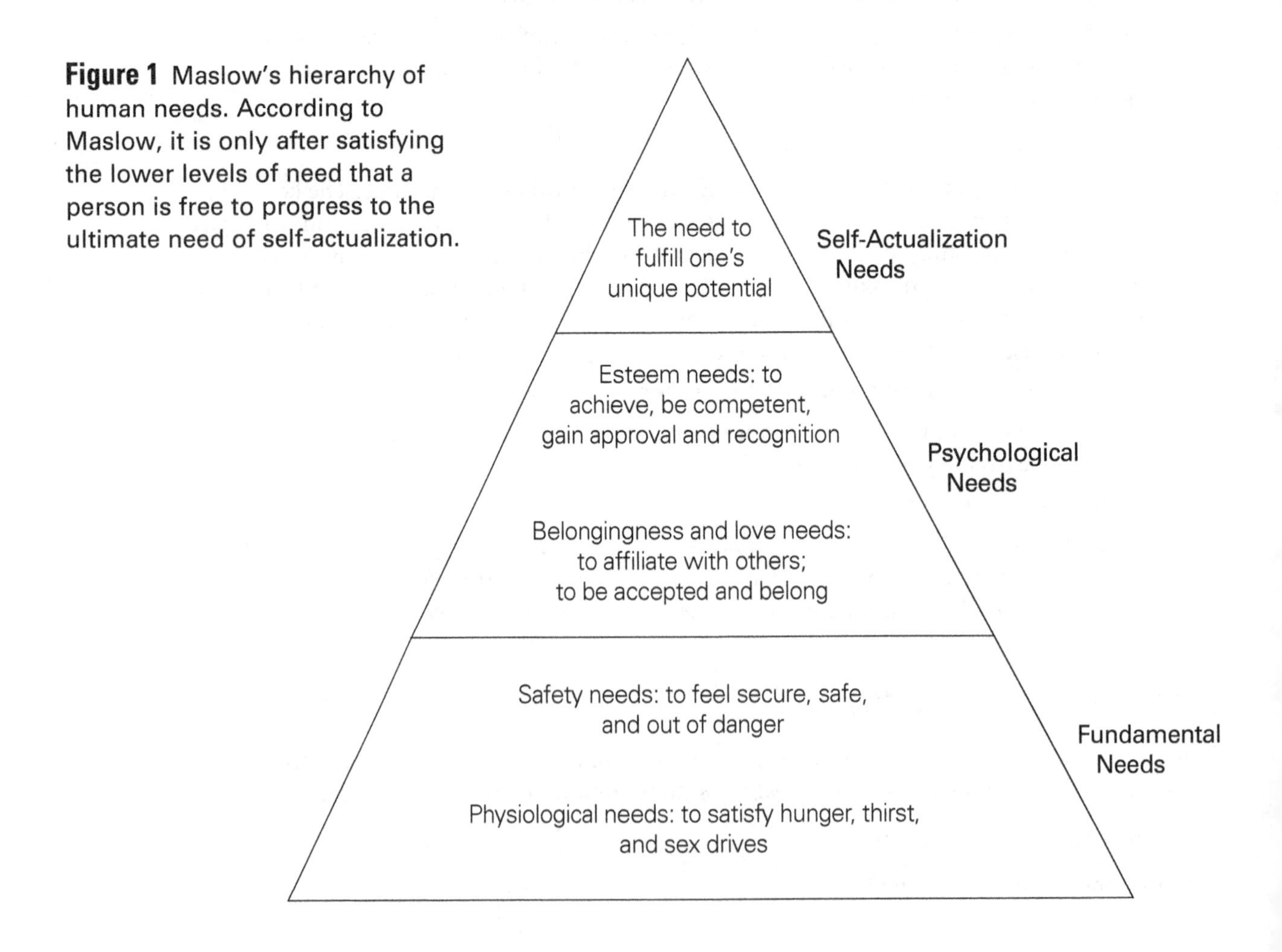

Figure 1 Maslow's hierarchy of human needs. According to Maslow, it is only after satisfying the lower levels of need that a person is free to progress to the ultimate need of self-actualization.

sex) and our need to feel safe, then we have difficulty proceeding to the next level which involves our psychological needs. These in turn need to be fulfilled in order to reach the top which is our self-actualization needs. For self-actualized persons, problems become a means for growth. Wouldn't it be nice to view problems in this manner?

What Is the Difference between External and Internal Motivation?

1. *Internal Motivation*—These are motivational elements that are within ourselves. We have feelings of pleasure or disgust as we meet or fail to meet our own standards. This is the reinforcement level we should all strive to meet. We should try to find value in our work, enjoy success, develop an appropriate value system, and thereby reinforce ourselves for our efforts. People differ in what they think provides reinforcement.
2. *External Motivation*—These are motivational elements that come from outside stimuli. Rewards in the form of material things, privileges, recognition, trophies, praise, or friendship. These are a "public" way of saying a job is well done.

CRITICAL THINKING

Todd felt he had prepared for his first major exam in geology. Science was difficult for him. He had attended all lectures, revised his notes, and read the chapters. He made an appointment with his professor to clarify some points that he didn't understand. He felt he was ready for the exam. When Dr. Jones returned the test, Todd had scored 94%. The reward of the high score was a real high! He felt successful, and knew he could continue to do well in this course. He called his parents that night and they were elated. Their praise echoed their feelings. Todd had received internal and external praise. Do you believe the external or the internal motivation that he received from the test score was the best motivator?

As you progress through school, internal motivators should become stronger. We should not always feel the need for external motivation. This doesn't mean we don't want external rewards, but its value should begin to lessen.

WHAT ARE YOUR GOALS?

Motivation is the first step in all goals. A goal should be something that you desire and that you will be motivated enough to try and reach.

Goals can be divided into three categories:

1. *Personal*—These will be determined by your value system. You have already filled out the Value exercise. This should give you an idea of what you feel is important to you. Personal goals can also include personal fitness, developing a positive attitude, and overcoming a bad habit.

2. *Academic*—You can be successful if you set your goals on what you want to get out of college. The exercise on reasons to attend college should also include some academic goals.
3. *Work Related*—What do you want from your chosen field of work? Improving your performance? Changing jobs? Learning new skills?

Why Do You Need Short-Term and Long-Term Goals?

It is necessary to have short-term and long-term goals. It is easy to lose motivation with only long-term goals. Short-term goals are necessary to act as our motivational elements. The accomplishment of these goals give us the will to succeed. Long-term goals clarify our direction.

What Are Some Important Characteristics of Goals?

There are four characteristics of goals that we will discuss. While you are reading about these characteristics, think about how you can apply these points to your life.

1. *Goals should be realistic*—A realistic goal is one you can reasonably expect to achieve given your abilities. If your goal is too high and you don't reach it, it can certainly affect your self-concept. If your goal is too low, when you attain this goal there is no real feeling of success.

   Amy attained a 3.0 (out of a 4.0) in high school. Her college goal was to attain a 3.0 average. Is this a realistic goal? Is Amy setting herself up for failure, or is this a possible goal?

   Bill was valedictorian of his graduating class. His goal in college was to maintain a C average. His goal was not high enough to give him the sense of accomplishment that he would need to make him feel successful.
2. *Goals should be measurable*—A measurable goal establishes a time frame and it also has a foreseeable outcome. You should have daily and weekly goals. Attaining these short-term goals will give you the successful feeling that you need to experience to keep you going. Semester, yearly, and other long-term goals (college degree, marriage, family) are also vital because they clarify your direction.
3. *Goals should be flexible*—Decide what you want to do and be willing to change your plans if necessary. Rarely do we set goals and follow through to completion without any problems. You might change your major, withdraw from a class, or experience any number of setbacks. Reassess your plan for reaching your goal. You might need to revise it or make a new plan. It's alright to change your goals if you make a mistake or decide to change your plans.
4. *Goals should be specific*—The purpose of goals is to make us "act." In order for a goal to activate us, we must have specific objectives in mind. If we are too vague, we never receive the satisfaction of success that we should feel when we attain the goal.

   Nancy's goal this semester is to attain a 3.0 grade point average. Peggy's goal this semester is to "do well" in her classes. Who will receive the greater satisfaction if they attain their goal? Who will know if their goal is met?

CRITICAL THINKING

Your long-term goal is to be a lawyer. Is that enough to motivate you to attend and be excited about the basic psychology class that you have at 8:00 a.m. on Monday, Wednesday, and Friday? Maybe at first, but as the semester rolls along there will be mornings that being a lawyer doesn't quite have the zip that it once did. The short-term goal of making a B in psychology that will complete three hours of general education requirements just might! (Hopefully your short-term goal will be to learn as much as you can about human behavior so you can effectively deal with people in your law practice.) It will help you to have a goal that you can accomplish in a short period of time to serve as an inspiration. An even better short-term goal would be to make a B on the first exam. Once this is accomplished, hopefully the adrenaline will flow!

Goals do not have to be major events. Your goal for today may include:

Pick up cleaning

Read Chapter 3 in sociology

Do math problems 2.1 through 2.6

Clean the bathroom

These are specific goals. You will know at the end of the day if you have attained them. These are much more motivating than:

Run errands

Study

Catch up on housework

IS THERE A RELATIONSHIP BETWEEN SETTING GOALS AND ACADEMIC SUCCESS?

After what we have learned to recognize about goals, this is an easy question to answer—Yes—Yes—Yes. Goals are activators, they provide a successful background that enables you to continue to strive. They are like gas to a car, food to our bodies, and rain to the grass.

The attainment of goals is also related to a positive attitude and high self-esteem. When we attain goals, we feel successful!

HOW CAN YOU DEVELOP A POSITIVE ATTITUDE?

Visualize yourself being successful. Jeni Burnett, a Pittsburgh State University basketball player, relates her success technique at the free throw line:

> *First of all, I block out the crowd noise. I dribble a couple of times and feel the ball. During this time I visualize my entire body. I think about my legs bent properly, my arms' and hands' position, my release, the ball being "up," the correct spin, the right arch, my follow-through. I see the ball "swish" the net.*

It is amazing how powerful positive thinking can be! It is also very contagious. Of course, negative thinking is also contagious. It is unbelievable how a "down" person can pull others "down" with them. We all know some people that constantly dwell on the negative side of life. They sometimes do not even realize it—it has become a way of life.

> *Fred woke up with a headache. He had worked a double shift the previous day. His roommate, Jim, was on his way out the door to class. Jim had actually read his history chapter and he hoped it would help him take better notes. Fred noticed it was raining; he had worked a double shift the previous day. He rolled over and muttered that he wasn't going to fight the rain to listen to Dr. Smith's boring biology lecture. It was annoying enough that he had a headache. He could have gotten the notes from Sue, but he recalled after his remark about her sweater that she probably wouldn't share her notes. He told Jim that he couldn't understand why teachers always seem to enjoy frustrating students. There had to be more to life. Jim walked out the door to go to class. He was beginning to wonder why he got out of bed today.*

WHAT ABOUT THAT NEGATIVE VOICE?

Should we look at the negative side of a situation? We don't like to because being a "positive" person is crucial to our success. We also need to be realistic (unfortunately or fortunately—life is "real"). What are you going to do if you fail the first test in one of your classes? That is a possibility (distant, of course). What will your plan be? Inside we have two voices that are always screaming to get out of us. One is a positive voice, the other is the dreaded negative voice. Unfortunately, the voice seems to have more volume at the most inopportune times.

> *Jane came to college from a large high school. She took college prep classes and maintained a B average. She was active in a lot of social activities in her high school. Studying was a concern, but certainly not a major one. She kept up in her classes with very little effort. Jane came to college and since she had experienced success in high school with very little effort, why should this change? The social scene was important to her in college (that's o.k.) and she knew everything would just fall in place. In sociology and biology her first exams fell on the same day. (Don't teachers ever get together and try to avoid this?) The night before the tests (as in high school), Jane sat down and started digging. "Surely, I won't need to know all of this, so I'll concentrate on my notes," she rationalized. "The notes are obviously what the teachers will think is important. After all, that is what they talked about!" A lot of the information didn't seem that vital, so Jane picked out what she thought would be on the tests. About midnight, after telling at least twelve of her friends how hard she was studying, she was ready to call it a night. After all, her biology test was at 11:00 and her sociology was at 1:00. There was a mild panic at 9:30 the next morning when she realized she had slept through her alarm. But, not to worry, she had plenty of time to shower and review once more. Food could wait until lunch.*

The biology test was given to the class. How could it be that many pages? Where did he come up with these questions? She found a lot of questions that she thought she knew, but the wording was ridiculous! What a relief when that was finished! On for a quick lunch and the sociology test.

She thought, "These teachers must get together and decide to ask weird questions." She wondered if there was an upper level education class for teachers that taught them to ask sneaky questions. "Why don't they ask questions that come directly from the book? After all, they wanted us to read it."—were two thoughts that Jane had. Jane definitely needed a nap after these two tests. She wasn't very concerned until the tests were handed back. There must be a mistake! She had never made a D in her life! How could she have made a D on both exams? She quickly folded back the corner of the tests so no one could see. What voices were screaming to be heard?

This could and might very well happen to you. It's not important that it happened, but it's how you are going to react that is important. You can turn this experience into a productive event. Before you throw this book in the trash, let's analyze the situation. Which voices will be dominant?

"I'm not smart enough to be here!"

"The teacher is a jerk—he didn't cover this!"

"He tried to trick us!"

"I hate this class!"

"At least I did better than Sally."

"I didn't really understand, I just memorized."

"I could have used the book to help me understand the notes."

"Now I know the type of questions that he asks."

High school students are usually concerned with the "literal" meaning of their textbooks. This means they are interested in the exact meaning—the words that are obviously stated. In college it is important to have an understanding of the material so you can *apply* the information. Concepts or ideas should be the result of studying your text. Maybe this means one of our *goals* should be the understanding of what the author is trying to say along with your teacher's interpretation. What do you think?

SUMMARY

It is important to think about *why* you are attending college. You should recognize your values and goals because they clarify your direction. Your motivation is directly related to achieving your goals. Success in our endeavors strengthens our will to succeed.

A good positive attitude is vital in achieving success in college as well as in life!

NAME: ______________________ DATE: ______________

EXERCISE 1. WHY ARE YOU HERE?

What are your reasons for attending college? Listed below are some reasons why some students attend college. Check those which are closest to the reasons why you are here.

_______ 1. I want to earn a degree.

_______ 2. My friends are in college and I want to be with them.

_______ 3. I want to please my parents.

_______ 4. I want to meet new people.

_______ 5. I want to prepare myself for a career.

_______ 6. College graduates make more money.

_______ 7. I want to broaden my knowledge.

_______ 8. College graduates have more status.

_______ 9. I don't want to work full time.

_______ 10. I want to improve my skills so I can get a better job.

_______ 11. My parents gave me no other choice.

_______ 12. I have a strong desire to achieve.

_______ 13. I want to become more independent.

_______ 14. I wanted to get away from home.

_______ 15. I want to participate in campus social life.

_______ 16. I have an athletic scholarship, veteran's benefits, etc.

_______ 17. College graduates have better jobs.

_______ 18. I couldn't go when I was younger.

_______ 19. I can advance to a higher level position at work.

_______ 20. To help ensure success in life.

_______ 21. I want to please my family.

_______ 22. I want to provide a good role model for my children.

_______ 23. I am being retrained because I lost my job.

List 5 of your reasons in order of priority (1 = highest priority).

1. ______________________________

2. ______________________________

3. ______________________________

4. ______________________________

5. ______________________________

NAME: ______________________________ DATE: ____________________

EXERCISE 2. VALUES

In the first column check 10 of the values that are most important to you. In the second column, rank from 1–10 the order of priority of these 10 values.

Value	Check	Rank
A world without prejudice	______	______
A satisfying and fulfilling marriage	______	______
Lifetime financial security	______	______
A really good love relationship	______	______
Unlimited travel opportunities	______	______
A complete library for your use	______	______
A lovely home in a beautiful setting	______	______
A happy family relationship	______	______
Good self-esteem	______	______
Freedom to do what you want	______	______
An understanding of the meaning of life	______	______
Success in your chosen profession	______	______
A peaceful world	______	______
Recognition as the most attractive person in the world	______	______
A satisfying religious faith	______	______
Freedom within your work setting	______	______
Tickets and travel to any cultural or athletic event as often as you wish	______	______
The love and admiration of friends	______	______
A chance to direct the destinies of a nation	______	______
International fame and popularity	______	______
The ability to eliminate sickness and poverty	______	______
A month's vacation with nothing to do but enjoy yourself	______	______

Write a brief paragraph describing what goals you are setting for yourself that reflects your top value choices.

NAME: ______________________ DATE: ______________

EXERCISE 3. THE COAT OF ARMS

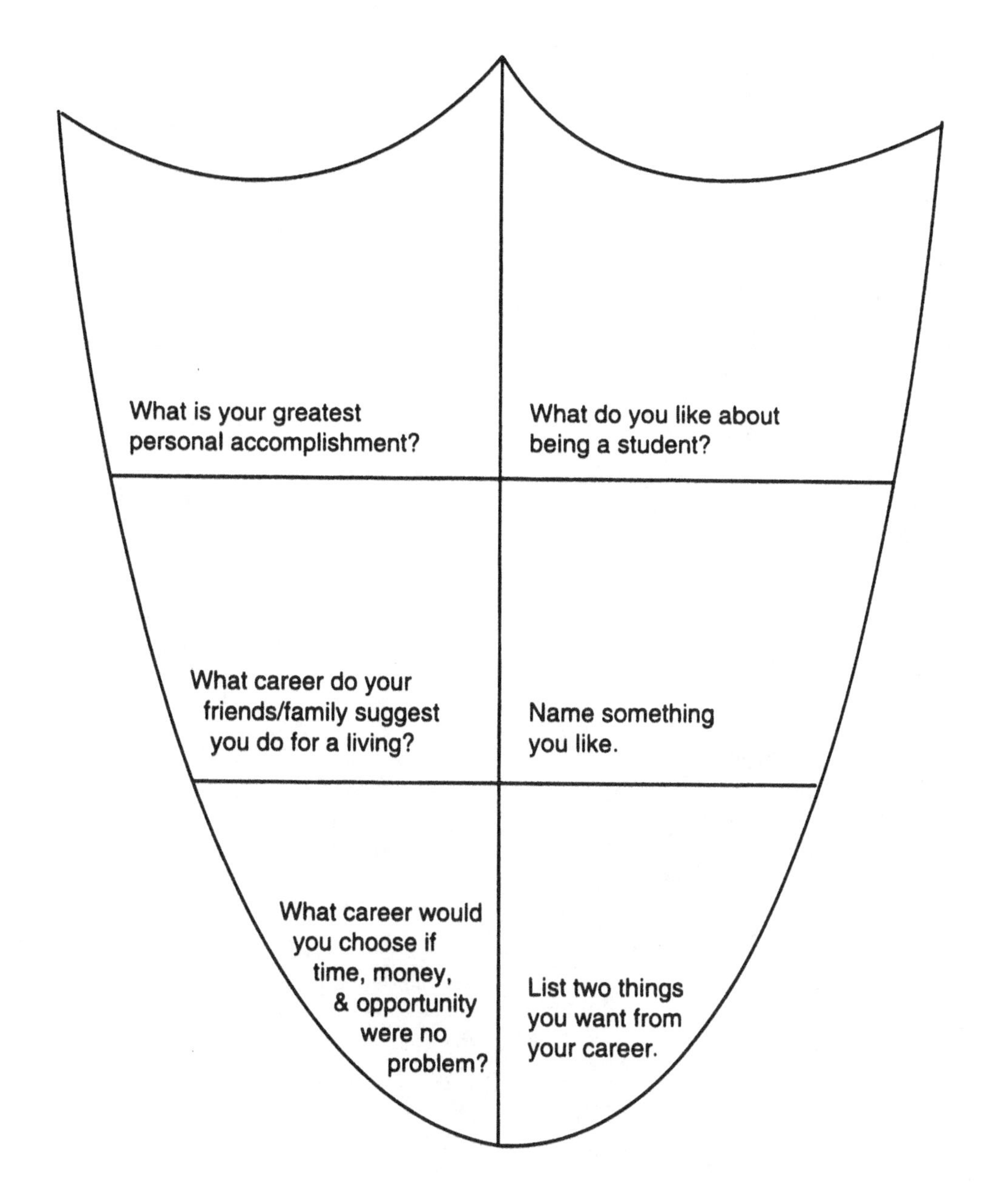

NAME: ______________________________ DATE: ____________________

EXERCISE 4. PERSONAL GOALS

Your responses must meet the established criteria for goals!

Semester/quarter goals: ______________________________

____

____

____

Mid-term goals: ______________________________

____

____

____

One-year goals: ______________________________

____

____

____

Monthly goals: ______________________________

____

____

____

NAME: ______________________________ DATE: ____________________

EXERCISE 5. EXTERNAL OR INTERNAL MOTIVATION?

Considering your experience in classes that you have taken, what has motivated you to learn, to work, to achieve?

In the first column, put a check mark if the experience has been used to motivate you. In the second column, decide whether the motivation was *E* (external motivation) or *I* (internal motivation).

_____ _____ 1. Teacher paying attention to me

_____ _____ 2. Not wanting to disappoint the teacher

_____ _____ 3. Getting on the honor roll

_____ _____ 4. Getting a job in the future

_____ _____ 5. Wanting to learn and understand

_____ _____ 6. Parents caring about me

_____ _____ 7. Teacher caring about me

_____ _____ 8. My satisfaction from receiving a high grade on an exam

_____ _____ 9. Not wanting to disappoint parents

_____ _____ 10. Being praised by classmates

_____ _____ 11. Finally figuring out the correct answer

_____ _____ 12. Putting words together that became concepts that made sense

_____ _____ 13. Helping other students

_____ _____ 14. Pleasing my family

List below the latest internal motivator that you have experienced.

____

List below the latest external motivator that you have experienced.

____

Write a brief paragraph describing how you feel you became motivated. Do internal or external motivation factors seem to be the most important? Do you feel motivated at this time of your life? Why?

____

____

____

____

____

____

____

____

____

____